WRITING FICTION

R. V. CASSILL is the author of many short stories and articles, as well as eighteen novels, including *Doctor Cobb's Game, The Goss Women, Clem Anderson, The President,* and *Pretty Leslie.* He has taught in writer's workshops at Columbia, Harvard, Purdue, Iowa, and Brown, as well as in several short-term writer's conferences.

WRITING FICTION

Second Edition

R. V. CASSILL

A FIRESIDE BOOK
Published by Simon & Schuster
New York London Toronto Sydney Tokyo Singapore

F

FIRESIDE
Simon & Schuster Building
Rockefeller Center
1230 Avenue of the Americas
New York, New York 10020

First Fireside Edition 1992

Published in 1986 by Prentice Hall Press
Originally published by Prentice-Hall, Inc.
FIRESIDE and colophon are
registered trademarks of Simon & Schuster Inc.

Manufactured in the United States of America

20   19

Library of Congress Cataloging-in-Publication Data
Cassill, Ronald Verlin (date).
Writing fiction
1. Fiction-Technique.   2. Short Stories
I. Title.
PN3355.C3   1975   808.3   75.12535
ISBN 0-671-76585-X

To all my teachers and all my students

I might not tell everybody,
but I will tell you.

WALT WHITMAN

CONTENTS

Section Two

THE STORIES

Section Three

THE CONCEPTS OF FICTION

AUTHOR TO READER

In this revised edition I have retained much of the text that has been, I am told, useful to very many young writers. Since the book was first published in 1963, I have added twelve years to my experience as a teacher and writer, as book reviewer and adviser to publishers. So now that experience covers a full quarter of a century. My fundamental ideas and devotion to the art of fiction have not changed. More than ever I believe in its importance as a means for seeing life whole. It is a bulwark against the transitory inflation and distortion of opinions kindled by the dispensers of unassorted "facts"; and if fiction itself is subject to fashions, fads, and the exploitation of partisan cliques, nevertheless it remains a refuge for those who want to explore the human condition as sentient men and women.

I remain convinced that an apprentice in the art must seek in reading the techniques within which he may give form to his own observations. The young writer must persist in comparing his work with the publications of more experienced authors. Therefore, this book emphasizes analytical reading as an integral part of learning to write fiction.

The short stories included here were chosen to illustrate—as well as so few stories can—a variety of approaches to the task of fitting a tale to its appropriate form. They can serve as models useful to you in measuring your own accomplishment. With pride I point out that two of these are by former students of mine, Joy Williams and Mark Costello. In this period of sometimes frenzied agitation about the prominence and role of women, it may be necessary to remark that, though Joy Williams' is the only work by a woman in this collection, there are multitudinous novels and stories by women that could have served as well for examination, discussion, and emulation.

I recommend that you read the stories for pleasure before you buckle down to analyzing them. It might suit you to read them all before you begin my first chapter. But I want to leave that to your whim or discretion—along with all the other practices and approaches I recommend. I think a teacher must offer possibilities and alternatives, not prescriptions. I would rather encourage, as best I can, whatever personal enthusiasms or penchants you begin with.

In any case, you'll find in continuing through my chapters of comment that reading the stories once is not sufficient. You should return to them often enough to be really familiar with them, so that when we examine a few lines from any one of them, you'll recall how that passage is related to the whole story.

I have not prescribed any particular projects to be completed in conjunction with the reading of my text. My assumption is merely that while you're reading you are also working on stories or a novel. I can promise that some of the things I have to say will mean more and will probably be clearer to you if you are actually at work on your own fiction than if you are merely thinking about making a start. Hopefully, this book will still have something to say to you months or years after you first open it, for I have touched on some of the subtlest problems of the art as well as many of the fundamental ones.

In general I have attempted to follow a progressive line of complexity, starting with relatively simple matters and ending with the more difficult, but you'll find that the late chapter on Theme returns to the same concerns as the early one on Choosing a Subject. It is not a duplication of the earlier chapter but a more probing examination of the sources of imagination from which the creative act emerges. I make no apologies for this doubling back. It is intentional—and intended to imitate the natural progress of the writer, which must always be cyclic.

As you go on writing you will make an endless series of spirals over familiar landscapes, until at last the familiar takes on the wonderful novelty of something you yourself created, something that did not exist before you gave it a fictional form.

I hope that what I have to say may be useful to the writer working alone. I hope, too, that it may serve teachers and students of writing who work together in a group. In trying to be as flexible, yet thorough, as I could be, I have included some observations for the beginner and some for the very competent writer. For the latter I would like to put in a caution not to glide too hastily over fundamentals. I think that really accomplished professionals—like great athletes—must return constantly to basic principles, disciplines, and even exercises.

Becoming a good writer is not easy. No process of training can guarantee it. Those who disparage any kind of instruction in fiction writing have a point when they say you can't make a silk purse out of a sow's ear. In my experience, though, it has turned out that very few sow's ears want to become silk purses. Most people who want to write have some correct intuition of fineness in themselves and a correct intuition that learning the disciplines of the craft is a good way to expose and measure that fineness.

It never occurred to me that mere acceptance of the ideas in this book would guarantee any results whatever. I cannot promise to make you into a professional writer or even a good writer. What I do believe is that what I propose may help you organize and effectively advance the talents for observation and expression that you already possess.

The only promise I can make is this: Every increase in the scope of your talent that you earn by responsible work will justify the effort that it cost. Writing is a way of coming to terms with the world and with oneself. The whole spirit of writing is to overcome narrowness and fear by giving order, measure, and significance to the flux of experience constantly dinning into our lives. Out of that din come fear of ignorance, fear of being alone, fear of dying without having defied the brutal indifference of the physical universe. Everyone who writes makes some attempt to face those fears by the very act of writing as best he can.

The writer who sticks loyally to his art and craft has a better chance than most to liberate himself from that apathy that is a prime contemporary symptom of cowardice. He cares. He learns the value of caring by the stewardship of his talent—by following it as it leads him through experience that many people would shun.

So whatever else this book may do for you, I hope it will guide you past the point of being afraid to try—with everything you have, with educated judgment, without hesitation—for success as a writer.

WRITING FICTION

THE MECHANICS OF FICTION

1

READING AS A WRITER

If you're awfully impatient to get to work, I can tell you now *exactly* how a story is made. It is made by uttering a declarative statement—"Joe wrote Maureen a dishonest, flattering letter"— and answering the questions naturally provoked by such a declaration: Who is Joe? Who is Maureen? What involvement have they with each other that motivates Joe to write a dishonest letter?

These questions will be answered by further declarations, which in turn require explanations. If you keep on giving explanations, presently you will have a story—of sorts.

This is exactly how all fiction is made. In the beginning there is an utterance. Then there is explanation.

However, like any "exact" formula in the arts, this none-too-serious prescription leaves a great deal to be said. To make it serious one must point out exhaustively how a writer learns *which* questions to ask, how they are best answered, and when enough has been said.

Certainly the writer can acquire technical principles otherwise than by distilling them from the fiction he reads. Yet reading remains essential because most technical concepts are learned more quickly and thoroughly from examples than from abstract definitions.

Consider this. It is generally agreed by modern critics and practitioners of fiction that nothing is more characteristic of the art than concreteness of expression. *Concreteness* ought to be your aim in all you write and revise. Very well, you say, but what is this concreteness?

It can be abstractly defined as the rendition of actions, people, places, and things in language that relates how they would be registered by an observer's senses of sight, sound, taste, smell, and touch. Concreteness is about the same as what Henry James called *realization*—the achievement of a sort of evoked reality from mere words.

Such an abstract definition is not without value. But keeping it in mind, read this passage from Flaubert's *Madame Bovary*:

> It was a fine summer morning. Silver gleamed in jewelers' windows, and the sunlight slanting onto the cathedral flashed on the cut surface of the gray stone . . . the square, echoing with cries, smelled of the flowers that edged its pavement—roses, jasmine, carnations, narcissus and tuberoses interspersed with well-watered plants of catnip and chickweed. The fountain gurgled in the center . . . bareheaded flower-women were twisting paper around bunches of violets.
>
> The young man chose one. It was the first time he had bought flowers for a woman; and his chest swelled with pride as he inhaled their fragrance, as though this homage that he intended for another were being paid, instead, to him.

Note, in the first paragraph, how many senses are appealed to in this realization of a summer morning in a French city. The gleam of silver and the sunlight on the cathedral illustrate the visual sensations; the gurgling fountain and the cries of merchants and customers appeal to the sense of hearing; the flowers and the wet plants stir the reader's recollection of actual smells.

Then, in the second paragraph, we see a young man in the midst of this color, sound, and smell. Within the quoted passage this young man is not described, characterized, or even named. Yet he is as real as fiction can make him, because here he serves as a focal point for all the sense impressions set loose by the previous paragraph. We cannot, of course, quite smell, or see, or hear this busy city square. (Unlike the theater or the movies, fiction can't rely on immediate sensual impact.) But we are induced to imagine that the young man is literally assaulted through every sense—and it is the concreteness of the objective world acting on his mind and emotions that gives him his fictional reality.

An experienced writer, criticizing the work of an apprentice, is apt to say repeatedly, "Don't tell us what your character or scene is like. *Show* us." Certainly you can learn how to *show*, to make your story concrete, by studying this example from Flaubert. If you return to it twenty times, it will still have things to teach you.

But several examples are better than one. You ought to look for the same qualities of concreteness in the stories in this book.

Note the baptism section in "Taking Care," the flinging of gifts to the goat in "Us He Devours," and the description of Anna's home in "The Lady with the Pet Dog." And don't stop with the examples in this volume. Once you have learned what to look for, all your reading ought to be a search for the variety of technical means by which various writers achieve their ends.

In urging you to read, I am doing no more than reminding you that a writer has many teachers. Good writers are your real teachers of how to write fiction, and their novels and stories are the means by which they teach. We know that Flaubert taught one other writer in a formal sense of the word. He coached, criticized, and advised Guy de Maupassant for several years before allowing him to publish anything. But it is also true that, in a less formal and direct way, Flaubert has taught most of the good writers of the past century— all those who "read as writers" when they looked into *Madame Bovary.*

"Reading as a writer" differs in a number of ways from other readings of fiction. The ordinary, intelligent nonprofessional expects, quite rightly, that fiction will give him a kind of illusion that something meaningful is happening to characters who have become very interesting in a particular situation. He recognizes traits of character that resemble those he has observed in life. He finds recognizable values at stake in the action of the story. (Will Joe harm Maureen by his dishonest letter? Will Lambert Strethers achieve magnificence or lose his self-respect?) Whether those values are preserved or destroyed conveys some meaning to the reader about the world he shares with the author. This sort of communication between author and reader is fine. It is the primary justification for fiction.

But there is another sort of transaction going on when a critic pauses to analyze a work. The critic generally wants to determine where to place this particular story. What *kind* of fiction is it? Is it realism or parody or fantasy? If it is realism, is it kin to the realism of Conrad, or that of Dreiser? Does the psychological insight of the story conform to the revelations of Freud? Or is it, perhaps, more intuitive—closer to the intuitions of D. H. Lawrence? Is the style derivative or original? Is the form of the story adequate to the meanings the author tried to load onto it? The critic's way of reading fiction is a good way, too, and a very valuable approach for a writer. If he has time and opportunity, a young writer ought to supplement his writing program with classes in the analysis of contemporary fiction.

But what the writer wants to note, beyond anything that concerns even the critic, is how the story, its language, and all its parts have been joined together.

The writer will look at the way the opening sentences and paragraphs are constructed to put certain information immediately before the reader.

> A new person, it was said, had appeared on the esplanade; a lady with a pet dog. Dmitry Dmitrich Gurov, who had spent a fortnight at Yalta and had got used to the place, had also begun to take an interest in new arrivals. (Opening sentences of "The Lady with the Pet Dog.")

There is a watchmaker's precision evident in the form of this opening. The first sentence implies, without a direct statement, that the setting will be one in which rumor has the force of authority, that here people are to some extent free of custom and the rigidity of their family or social position. We will learn from reading farther into the story that Yalta, a resort city, is such a place as is implied. In this atmosphere of transience and rumor, it is common, though a bit odd nevertheless, that ladies should be identified by such superficial trivia as their possession of pet dogs.

The second sentence, which names the principal character,

develops our awareness of social fluidity in Yalta by its restrained, wry statement of how quickly one becomes an old-timer in a place where none stay very long.

Thus, from the very beginning Chekhov has begun to develop the peculiarities of the setting in which the love of Gurov and Anna will begin its unworldly flourishing.

Dramatic, concrete, and already ironic, Chekhov's opening draws the reader swiftly into the heart of the experience to be endured by his characters.

Noting the skill of such an opening, the writer who reads it must, *above anything else*, be aware that the story might have opened otherwise. For instance:

> In the year 1883, Dmitry Dmitrich Gurov was vacationing at Yalta. His wife and children had remained at the family home in Moscow. While on vacation it was his daily habit to take sweets at a café on the esplanade. The gossips whom he met there one day told him that a new arrival had attracted the attention of many idle vacationers. Her name was not known. They spoke of her as the lady with the pet dog.

The point I wish to emphasize is not that my alternative opening is inferior to Chekhov's—which it certainly is—but that such another possibility for a beginning exists. *A writer reading must be forever aware that the story exists as it does because the author chose his form from among other possibilities.* From this recognition of author's choice comes the key to understanding what is excellent in the fabrication of Chekhov's story or any other good work.

To the ordinary reader-for-pleasure it ought to seem that the story is told in the language he finds on the printed page because it *has* to be told in just those words. As soon as we know better than that, we are reading as writers.

It is not always easy to understand why the author made the choice he did. For instance, why did Chekhov choose to caricature Gurov's wife as an intellectual shrew instead of picturing her as becoming pathetic as she grows older? That other choice would have served the purposes of the story—but it might have required greater development of her character, thus changing the proportions and center of interest

We cannot be sure how this other possible choice would have fitted. But mere speculation on it should make us realize that *no choice of character, action, language, names, or anything else is an isolated one.*

Each successive choice made as the writing progresses has to be made with respect for what has already been established. This is a respect for what I will call the overall unity of fiction. Suffice it to say for now that when you read as a writer you will keep asking how did the author harmonize A with B and B with C and C with D—on through a very long series of decisions that finally resulted in the story as we have it. We can't understand all the secrets of unifying a story at once. But the recognition of author's choice stimulates a fruitful curiosity.

For an example of another particular a writer ought to look for in his reading, let us recognize the obvious truth that characters in fiction have to be developed as the story rolls along. No character can be fully revealed the moment he is brought on the scene. They are developed by encountering situations in which they act to reveal themselves and act on other characters to affect the outcome of the story.

So one ought to note what sort of occasions in a story extend and amplify the first impressions given of each of the characters. How large an opportunity for character revelation is provided by the particular few situations that constitute any one story?

For a modest approach to understanding how a limited number of situations can reveal as much about character as they do, let's start with a recognition that they were contrived or chosen by the author exactly because of their capacity to expose significant qualities in his characters. We should ask constantly whether another set of circumstances would have served this purpose better or worse, remembering that in the writing, alternative choices could have been made.

In most stories that cover any span of time greater than several minutes, we are aware that only a part of the action that might have been given in detail has been fully presented. Why did the author omit some bits of dialogue that might, in actuality, have been spoken? How has the author covered the gaps that he chose to leave? Has he left some important realities up to the imagination of the reader? Of course he has, unless he is a real bumbler. But a skilled author will have chosen ways to make sure the reader imagined something consistent with what is given, rather than something irrelevant.

And while the author was contriving so many clever joints and putting in so many bolts, hinges, and braces, what else was he doing? Why, he was taking pains to hide all his carpentry work for the sake of the illusion he wants to give the reader.

Perhaps the last thing you need to find out, reading as a writer, is how an author has managed to disguise his own presence, how he has kept the curtain always between himself and the reader.

A writer must read, then, with close concentration. But, a writer also ought to read widely. What becomes of concentration and close attention to detail when one tries to plunge through a lot of stories, novels, and other reading matter in a short lifetime? Well, obviously there have to be occasions when he reads hastily, avidly, skipping like a stone flung across a pond. There's no need to be afraid this reading is wasted. Thomas Mann's *The Magic Mountain* and James Joyce's *Ulysses* are novels that might reward months or years of concentrated effort. But I suppose it is better (just a *little* better) to have dipped into one or the other during an afternoon's bus ride than never to have opened them at all.

The short stories printed in this book were chosen in the conviction that each, in its own special way, would be worth close examination. Most of them will be referred to in more than one chapter, implying you ought to return to each of them for more than one reading. Each time you read, I hope you'll learn something new.

Read poetry. Nowhere are there such possibilities of language on display as there are in poetry. Not all these possibilities are suitable for fiction, but the fiction writer ought, by all means, to know that they exist. Furthermore, some of the finest and most subtle narrative forms are found in poetry. Read the ballads "Little Musgrove," "The Demon Lover," or "Lord Randall" for a tiny sample. Read William Morris's "The Haystack in the Floods," or

"Sir Gawain and the Green Knight," or Robinson Jeffers' "Thurso's Landing" if you want to see how wonderfully stories can be told in verse.

Read drama. It can be useful reading for a fiction writer. Contemporary fiction has borrowed a great deal from the literature of the theater. For economy and deftness in giving information to the reader—for learning how to *show* him instead of telling him what he has to know—we can find worthwhile examples in many plays. Beyond this—it ought to go without saying—means of character delineation have had to be worked out to a high degree of subtlety for the stage.

So read widely. Read good things when you can find them. But don't—if you really mean to master your craft—be afraid of soiling your mind by reading works not exactly of first rank. In my experience, students who purposely confined their college reading to "the best"—meaning Shakespeare, Dante, Cervantes, Dostoevsky, Melville, and Henry James; all great writers, all writers in an idiom no longer common—had more than usual trouble in developing for themselves a supple style that would express their own experience. Sometimes more of one's basic craft can be learned from second-rank work.

It has probably occurred to you that I have outlined a reading program that will take years to complete, a reading program with no outside limit. I'm afraid I have. Certainly I do not mean to suggest that all this reading should be done before you put paper in your typewriter and strike out boldly for yourself.

All I expect by now is that you have read this chapter and the story, "The Lady with the Pet Dog." The next chapter should be the signal to write a story of your own. When you've finished it, read some more fiction.

2

CHOOSING A SUBJECT

Often in fiction writing classes I have found that the beginning writer will show much better taste and sense in his reading preferences than in the choice of material to be used in his own work. He admires and reads with pleasure the fiction of Hemingway and Faulkner, Katherine Anne Porter and D. H. Lawrence, Stephen Crane and James Joyce—or stories like the ones included in this book.

But lo and behold, when he comes to writing his own first story, some mysterious folly leads him to choose a gaudy, sensational, and unfamiliar subject matter, something snatched from a tabloid or an old-fashioned adventure magazine. Instead of attempting to produce the genuine excitement of discovery that he himself has known in reading good fiction, he hopes to dazzle with the artificial fireworks of exotic situations, cardboard heroisms, billboard beauty, and dismaying "surprise endings." (These surprise endings generally depend on the writer's withholding information that should have been given in the first paragraph of the story—that the main character is male, or a baby, or a black, or a pet, when the reader has been teased into believing the character a female, a Don Juan, white, or merely a human being.)

I never quite understood why students should waste their time and mine on efforts so far off the right track. Sometimes I guessed that they might be afraid to discover how little of their own experience they had actually possessed, how little of their own lives they had grasped.

Certainly it is terrifying to sense that all one's life has flickered away like a landscape seen from a train window, or that what remains from the vanished past is sealed away in memory as if it were in a bank vault for which there is no key. But the choice of becoming a writer is the choice to face some fears, including the fear of being a hollow or a dull person with nothing to say.

There are many subtle psychological reasons why people do not like to measure themselves. But my best advice—and I cannot state it too strongly—is to face the fear of hidden embarrassments forthrightly and take the subjects for your first stories from your own life.

And don't, please, scan your life for those moments that seem most superficially colorful, nor the moments when more or less accidentally you were cast in the glamorous role of a character from a piece of sensational adventure fiction.

It may well be the case that once upon a time you were involved in a holdup and acquitted yourself like Dick Tracy in the face of danger. It may be that, for the moment, you *were* Dick Tracy instead of your good self. But however entertaining Dick may be in his proper place in the comic strip, he is not a useful character for the kind of fiction I want to encourage. Far better to write about yourself when you were most yourself—in love, and in love with things that vanish, as Yeats puts it.

But I am not recommending that, for a beginning, you sit down to turn out a fragment of literal autobiography. Autobiography is a special kind of writing that sometimes has a very high value. It isn't fiction, though, and you ought to plunge with determination into the effort to make fiction.

To make a story out of your own experience, you will almost certainly have to make a *composite* out of bits and pieces of reality gleaned in whatever place or period you can remember them. If you tried to make these pieces stay in the chronological order of your own life, that would be autobiography. In fiction you discard the actual, or chronological, order. The fragments from here and there are put together because they seem—according to the intent of your story—to fit together.

Reality suitable as a subject for a complete story seldom comes to us in single nuggets that require merely to be delivered to the reader in concrete, active, and sensuous prose. Rather, it may be well enough to start writing down a single autobiographical fragment—and then let the composite grow around that.

It is not necessary to see your whole subject before you begin to write. One of the nice things about writing is that the full scope of a subject begins to dawn on one after he starts to write. So once you have a glimpse of the subject, begin to put it on paper. Unless stubborn habits of fear and self-doubt are too strong, a flood of memory and imagination will begin. From the flood you will select the materials that show the reader what your subject means— answering the questions and showing the emotional quality of the event and its relation to the universal patterns of loss and triumph that pervade all our lives. On your first effort—or your second, or your tenth—it will occur to you that, after all, not much has been lost of anything you ever knew. It has merely been inaccessible, and the act of writing is a way to possess your own life.

If these exhortations to begin, plunge, throw yourself into the deep water of writing a story sound thin and general—and admittedly they are a bit premature; they will be given more substance by later chapters—remember that a writer simply does the best he can at any moment in his development, even when one part of his mind knows he is floundering badly.

But begin you must. If you don't begin until you have all the available theory in your mind, you may never get a story on paper. Moreover, it is three times as easy to absorb theory if you are making efforts of your own to which it can be related.

Not the least of the benefits to be expected by a writer from his reading is guidance in finding his own subject matter.

It must have happened countless times that a writer in the midst of reading has felt a quickening excitement as he realizes, *Something like this—but not quite like this—once happened to me.* His interest in the story before him illuminates some hitherto neglected area of his own experience, suggesting suddenly that it possesses an inherent interest that might be exposed by forming it into fiction.

With his memory jogged by someone else's tale—or a poem or a movie—the writer finds himself almost involuntarily flung into preparations for a new story of his own. Most of these impulses will come to nothing and that is all right. The imagination will—and should—make a hundred starts for every story that is carried to completion.

But if the suggestion that comes from reading does prove solid enough to be built on, the odd, nice thing about the process is that the story that emerges need have no great resemblance to the one from which it sprang. No particular effort is usually required to provide for originality in a story that germinated from someone else's effort. The writer may well have intuited a connection between his own proper subject and the one he has been reading about. This subtle relationship will not—in fact it can't—prescribe a similarity in the details of substance and form.

It's been said that there are, fundamentally, only two stories: Cinderella and Jack and the Bean Stalk. It is also said there are less than half a dozen primary myths which are repeated over and over and over in the numberless stories of our culture: the myth of Rebellion, the myth of Salvation, the story of Venus rising from the foam, the Prometheus legend, the triumph of Christ.

Without going into this matter of the universality of a certain few myths that may be built into all stories, we can at least say that, of course, the fundamental pattern of one story may be fleshed out with the concrete details of quite another story.

Look, for example, at the subject matter of Joy Williams's story "Taking Care." It is, specifically, the story of a mild and somewhat inept preacher who is obliged to support and sustain three generations of females in his family. Their problems are mysterious to him, but he does his devout best. He keeps the faith. He brings his wife home—into the "shining rooms" that he has cleaned for her return. He offers an image of stability to his errant daughter and sees to the health of his granddaughter.

The characters, situation, and the language of the story are Joy Williams's, and no one should try to steal these from her.

But in a broader sense, the subject is the victory of stubborn goodness over the chaos and corruption of the temporal world. It is the triumph of the spirit over mortality. This, obviously, is not a new subject. It is mine, yours—anyone's who wants it. There are a thousand ways for it to be written freshly, though it has been told a thousand times. The kind of recollection a writer must perpetually engage in will surely suggest a different way you might tell this ageless story.

Selection of subject matter is an imaginative act. Someone who lacks the fundamental imagination to see that a fist fight on a playground at dusk is more interesting than a group of children numbly watching television shouldn't try to be a writer. It was part of Hemingway's imagination to go to the bullfights in Spain and all the wars he could get to. Legwork is a part of imagination. You've got to go take a look at life. You must have a nose, not so much for news, but for those vital occasions that somehow embody your notion of what our life is like.

Never minimize the importance of selecting your subject. On the other hand, don't let your choice of subject become so difficult that it keeps you from setting to work. Remember that a clear view of one's subject often emerges as one writes, growing fuller and deeper as the writing digs it out of its camouflage. It is not often a mass of ingredients lying ready for assembly on the writer's desk.

Remember that perspective on experience is valuable in getting it into meaningful order. It is often the case that you can be too near a thing to see it whole and steadily. There are certainly handicaps in trying to write about a love affair in which you are presently engaged.

Handicaps exist, then, in choosing almost any part of your experience as an ideal subject, though it remains true that an apprentice should write about people, places, and events he knows well.

Accept the handicaps with the confidence that the subject of your first story need not be the subject of your final masterpiece. Stories about one's childhood may have this advantage—they lead a writer on to recapitulate in his growth as story teller his former growth as a person. His stories just *may* grow up along with him.

On the other hand, stories written on subjects closer to your present experience may open vistas backward to the rich, potent, and definitive revelations that only childhood is privileged to know. My story "In the Central Blue" was written after I had written a long novel about an American poet *(Clem Anderson)* and one about adultery *(Pretty Leslie)*. Both these novels have crucial flashbacks to childhood episodes that seem closely related to what I put into the short story.

In any case, once you have reveled and wrestled with your first subject, doing your best with it, you ought to take a deep breath and admit that it is only a beginning.

A writer must be a strangely divided creature. First he works with blind enthusiasm—then casts a cold, cold eye on what the enthusiasm brought forth. The cold and critical eye is just as necessary and just as much a part of writing as the enthusiasm.

A young writer can hardly help feeling that each story he writes is an ultimate measure of his insight and of what he has to express. Hasn't he been absolutely frank? Hasn't he recklessly committed everything his years have taught him to these pages? Isn't the subject that he has tugged out of his buried life with such anguish and humility all he has of himself to offer a world fully preoccupied with dangers and opportunities? And—that being the case—hadn't he better start looking outside himself for subject matter if he wants to go on writing?

The answer must be *No* to all these questions. What seems ultimate is truly only preparatory. Alps beyond Alps arise, sure enough. The "most important" subject most of us lug out of our youth when we begin to write fiction is usually a pale substitute or a camouflaging screen for the better subject lurking behind and beyond it. The search for your true subject will go on long after you have forgotten you read this book.

You cannot possibly see the truth of such a proposition by self-examination at any one stage. The careers of famous writers illustrate it, though, and the one good reason for granting them their fame is that they serve so well as illustrations. (Dear, patient, illustrious dead men. When they were young they never knew about themselves what we know now.)

I think we can see in F. Scott Fitzgerald's earlier novels *This Side of Paradise* and *The Beautiful and the Damned* that he is hunting, still somewhat blindly, for the Jay Gatsby and the Dick Diver who were to be his "real" subjects. The themes, the emotional recklessness, the sense of a precarious social equilibrium, and even the fate of the characters in the earlier books hint that Gatsby and Diver were already lurking in the dark fields of Fitzgerald's imagination, waiting for the writer's stubborn search to "turn the light on them," as he once put it.

The larger accomplishment of Thomas Mann shows about the same thing. All that is unfolded in the great novels *The Magic Mountain, Joseph and His Brothers,* and *Dr. Faustus* is present in embryo in Mann's earlier stories and novels. When they were written, it may very well be that the author felt he had run his imagination to the end of its tether.

So, for the time being, he had. Yet here is the wonderful part of it: Every early choice of subject matter and its exploitation can now be seen as an exploration, preparing and conditioning the author to come closer in his next attempt to his true subject.

We see James Joyce in the same way. (Perhaps this is true with nearly all great writers.) The subjects of his early stories in *Dubliners*—not to mention the technique and discipline of the language—are surely stations he had to pass through before he was in a position to see Leopold Bloom, the modern Ulysses, as the natural and appropriate subject for a full display of his talents. The novel *Ulysses*, we are told, was originally conceived as one of the series of stories that would make up *Dubliners*. Joyce must have been a little surprised—and happy, in the peculiar fashion of writers—to discover he had come home to his true subject in very much the way Ulysses returned to Penelope—or Leopold to Molly Bloom—after many wanderings.

The moral here is striking enough. Our cold eye sees, sometimes, that our subjects are of only private importance. As soon as we have learned something about our craft, we are tempted to turn from concentration on our own experience to the public world of great events—to write about spies and congressmen. But the first commandment is to go back stubbornly to our own fields. This time—and the next time and the time after that—we must turn them more deeply than before.

In the long run the reward for this may only be that the writer will discover who he really is. His own identity will be clarified as his ability to write of his own experience increases. And that, I think, is a benefit none of us should scorn. That alone ought to entitle writing fiction to a place in the curriculum of the liberal arts.

But beyond that, as one goes on—if he is lucky, stubborn, gifted, and clever enough to learn from partial successes as well as failures—a writer will find that private experience and public experience lose their distinction. The boundary line is rubbed out. At the level of myth they begin to blend into each other, and finally one may discover the common heart of humanity, and hope and doubt and triumph, beating in the subject matter that seemed at first glance to be merely personal experience.

When that happens—and beware! it is not common and never easy—there exists a writer worth everyone's respect, a man in possession of material only he has the privilege to expound.

3

DESCRIPTION, NARRATIVE PASSAGES, SCENES, AND DIALOGUE

Writing is not an impersonal act like adding a column of figures. It is an act of exposure. If the subject doesn't come from the writer's life, the central emotion does. A writer not yet secure in his craft may very well feel doubly exposed by what he has written. First of all, he has revealed a subject and attitudes that may have been long hidden from the rest of the world. Second, he has, perhaps, exposed his shortcomings as a writer, his inability to shape his material into a story that satisfies his own standards.

No wonder he sometimes disowns, sometimes hysterically overestimates, the value of his effort. That's natural enough, but one can't afford to give in to such feelings often or long. One has to learn to criticize his own work—and then revise.

The subsequent chapters may provide an antidote to a purely emotional appraisal of your own work. The reasonable analysis of fictional elements can lead to enlightened revision—and let me say sternly that the writer who will not revise is a nuisance to himself, his teacher, and to mankind at large. He is also missing what has always been for me the most gratifying part of writing.

While fear and trembling still disturb your judgment of your first draft, cast a cold eye on its mechanical characteristics before you make any rash decisions.

For convenience' sake I categorize the elements of fiction as *mechanical* or *conceptual.* Among the former, I place description, narration, scene, half-scene, transitions, and dialogue. The latter category, to be dealt with later, includes character, plot, tone, theme, and other things less susceptible to mechanical measure.

Different sorts of description and the function of description can be demonstrated pretty well without respect to whether those descriptions are good or bad in themselves. The same is true of other elements I call mechanical. When we talk about character and plot, though, we'll be forced to consider how well they have been conceived if we want to make sense.

DESCRIPTION may be defined as language employed to present directly the qualities of an object, a person, or a scene. The image thus presented is sometimes static, sometimes a transient part of the action of the story.

In the contemporary stories in this book you will not find the sort of static, impersonal description that was so characteristic of nineteenth–century fiction—the cataloguing of items in a room, the full physical description of a character, the camera eye rendition of a landscape on which an action is about to take place. Rather, the rendering of appearances is accomplished through the emotionally conditioned senses of a character, as in this passage from "Us He Devours."

> . . . she had awakened from the sleepless dawns of girlhood to hear the cruel roosters cry *blood, blood, bloooood* across the sties and pens and across the hen yard's dusty wallows. Often she lay in her bed, listening to the sounds of animals already awake; the snigger of boars or somewhere in the corner of a pasture the dry dirt-pawing hoof of her father's bull. The dirt, the droppings of turkeys and pea fowl, and the dung of sparrows on a beam under a barn's cave were always there, or were seen in memory only as a brown composite of wind and random dust flapping across barnyards.

Thus the environment is animated and vitalized and becomes part of the human crux of the action, as it would not if the author had given us an impersonal view of the woman's surroundings.

Descriptions may be categorized as concrete, figurative, and abstract. The distinction among these kinds depends partly on the language chosen, but also on the way the imagination of the author has seized on the reality of the object or person to be described. Nearly every piece of fiction will contain examples of all three kinds.

In "The Lady with the Pet Dog," we find these concrete descriptions: ". . . the water was a soft, warm lilac color, and there was a golden band of moonlight on it." And, "The theater was full. As in all provincial theaters, there was a haze above the chandelier, the gallery was noisy and restless." And, "Directly opposite the house stretched a long gray fence studded with nails."

These figurative descriptions: ". . . he thought how much angularity there was still in her laugh and manner of talking with a stranger." (The word *angularity* is used metaphorically, suggesting that the figure and movements of a young girl have their counterpart in her laughter and manner.) And, in the husband's buttonhole, "there was an academic badge like a waiter's number." (The simile adds a note of ridicule to the description of the husband's appearance.)

Abstract descriptions: ". . . in his character there was something attractive and elusive that disposed women in his favor and allured them." And, "He had two lives; an open one, seen and known by all who needed to know it, full of conventional truth and conventional falsehood, exactly like the lives of his friends and acquaintances, and another life that went on in secret."

Perhaps the main risk inherent in the use of abstract descriptions is that they may pass judgments on characters without allowing the reader to make up his own mind on the basis of evidence. This is called "author intrusion" and can very gravely weaken the sense of reality in fiction. Since concreteness is the soul of fiction, it would seem obvious that concrete descriptions are the safest, the most reliable. It is a good principle to make your reader "see, hear, and feel." Yet it would be foolish to rule out the use of abstract descriptions merely because they *can* be abused.

A sizable proportion of the descriptions in Chekhov's story are abstract—and this is quite proper because Gurov comes to face the quandaries of love through a series of intellectualized perceptions. The ingredients of morality and reason are fundamental to the meaning of the action here.

The function of descriptions in fiction is generally to deepen the illusion of person and place—to recreate their substance in the imagination of the reader, so that he is willing to believe he is in the presence of reality.

Another function is to mirror the emotional state of characters. The way the objective world is depicted hints at the mood of the people who inhabit it. A crude illustration of this can be given by saying that a description of night, fog, and cold will hint that the characters are miserable or depressed. Descriptions of meadows in May will hint at some bubble of happiness.

Somewhat more delicately shaded examples appear in Chekhov's story. In the first pages we get a description of the sea at Yalta. The sensuous attractiveness of the warm, lilac-colored water and the moonlight playing on it is keyed to Gurov's mood when he first meets Anna. At this time he is careless and indolent—ready to respond to superficial loveliness whether it appears in a human or other natural form.

Later, in the time when the frustrations and contradictions of love have caught him by the throat, it is very natural that his eye might linger (where that of the reader is skillfully directed by the author's description) on the shabby pomp of the provincial theater and the long gray fence studded with nails—a fence gray as the monotony of enforced separation and menacing as the social prohibitions against adultery.

So we see that descriptions of differing quality will serve to emphasize for the reader—like accent marks—the changes that have taken place in the characters and their situation. (A virtuoso performance in using the altering aspects of the exterior world to show the alterations of the psyche is Thomas Mann's *Death in Venice*. There the city in various weathers becomes "mirror and image" of the subconscious changes in the main character.)

Another means of description available to an author consists of having one character describe another. Thus, in "The Lady with the Pet Dog" Anna says, " 'My husband may be a good, honest man, but he is a flunkey!' "

What is accomplished by such indirect description that could not be done better in the author's own words? Certainly the good reader will expect the indirect to be less reliable, more *biased* than the direct.

That's it. The value of indirect description lies precisely in its revelation of bias. The description, as Chekhov uses it, shows the wife's "access of bitter feeling"—and has also given us a view of the husband's character that may be accepted tentatively while we wait for it to be confirmed or refuted.

By shedding some light on two characters—speaker and person he describes—indirect descriptions kill two small birds with one small stone. And in the tight confines of a short story, the writer has to search constantly for ways to achieve economy.

Further, this sort of indirect description contributes to the lifelikeness of fiction. Frequently we hear about people before we meet them and have a chance to judge them for ourselves. By what we hear we are predisposed to like or dislike them. Then when our own direct impressions of these people force us to a reappraisal of expectations, we find ourselves at the point of conflict between authorities. However mild that conflict may often be, it is the very stuff of drama. Much of the celebrated "dramatic" method of Henry James is an exploitation of the conflict between expectation and discovery.

TRANSITIONS. Since the texture of fiction ought to be consistent, and a story ought to progress with a smooth flow from one passage to the next, you will want to watch for the means various authors use to move from description to narrative, from narrative to scene.

To move from a static description, the classic transition is provided by having someone act on whatever has been described. (If the author has described a melon, someone cuts a slice out of it. If he has described a pool, someone dives into it. After which, Someone becomes the center of interest.)

You might turn back once more to the passage from *Madame*

Bovary. Note that the transition from description to action is made by having the young man enter the square and choose a flower from one of the flower stands. After the stillness of the picture is disturbed, the author can proceed smoothly to telling us about the young man and about how he feels.

"Murphy's Xmas" should be studied very carefully to discern how the author manages a whole series of dazzling transitions—from one time to another, from place to place, from the general to the particular, from the subjective to the visible objective and from concrete language to rarified metaphor. This is a virtuoso performance that would require a very long analysis to explicate fully. If, at first glance, you think that his transitions are merely capricious, keep looking until you realize how responsible they are. Some devices have been borrowed from cinematography, some from the inventions of modern poets.

NARRATIVE PASSAGES are those parts of fiction which condense action into its largest movements. They are long–range views in contrast to the detailed close-ups of action and characters given in scenes. Narrative passages may telescope the events of several years into a few small paragraphs or less, while the time it takes to read a full scene is roughly comparable to the time it would require to be enacted.

There is no end to the variety possible in the composition of narrative passages. The examples given here are not intended to illustrate the full range of possibility but only to fix general characteristics in your mind. Henceforward in your reading of fiction, be on the lookout for varieties of usage. You'll find there is a special pleasure—as well as advantage—in an awareness of the mechanical design in fiction.

In "The Lady with the Pet Dog" the first several paragraphs of Section III constitute an uninterrupted narrative. The constant and repeated experiences of several months are depicted as a single bloc of action from which emerge no specific occasions having anything to do with the center of interest. We are told that the image of Anna did not fade as Gurov had expected it to. We are *not* given an instance of his summoning that image to mind or reliving his memories in detail, though such an instance might have had considerable dramatic force. The realism of the story would not have been violated by its inclusion. But the principle of economy probably ruled it out.

Since economy is nearly always an issue in the short story, we can see why the compression of time and action into narrative passages may often be useful. The novel doesn't impose such strict demands for economy, but there the choice to present certain things in narrative may be used to change the pace, to subordinate the sequences of lesser interest, and to summarize when the reader has already been given all the detailed views he needs.

The narrative of Section III serves as a bridge—as narrative passages usually do—between the scenes at Yalta and the scenes in the provincial town to which Gurov goes in search of Anna. The routine of this protracted period is given considerable concreteness even though the view is a long-range one. "When the first snow falls, on the first day the sleighs are out, it is pleasant to see the white earth, the white roofs; one draws easy, delicious breaths. . . ." "When in the evening stillness the voices of his children preparing their lessons reached his study, or when he listened to a song or to an organ playing in a restaurant, or when the storm howled in the chimney, suddenly everything would rise up in his memory. . . ."

The author has managed to compress time without abandoning concreteness. He does this by choosing for the passage sensuous details that are recurrent through the period he is telling about. He has also adapted his verbs and time modifiers to express the sense that rich and detailed life is going on, though so far away from our point of observation that we can only guess at the vast majority of details.

While narrative passages generally appear as links between the more scenic parts of a fictional work, they also serve sometimes to get a story started. In the long perspective of narrative we are given the main outlines of a situation and an action that has been developing over an extended period. Then, when the author has satisfied us that the action is approaching a climax, he shifts to closer range and the illusion thenceforward is that we are observers at the scene itself. So narrative may also be thought of as a transitional phase preparing the reader's interest until he is ready to accept the illusion of a pure scene. It conditions him, sometimes, for a "willing suspension of disbelief" by requiring, first of all, only as much suspension as is necessary to accept some generalized information about the way human affairs commonly run.

In any case, narrative passages normally progress into scenes. Section III of the Chekhov story begins with narrative, moves on into a scene.

The transition is marked by the words, "One evening. . . ." That means, in the sense of the story, "on one of those evenings that altogether have constituted the whole period covered by the preceding narrative." It is a mechanical signal to the reader that now we are going to get down to the scene itself and he had best be ready to accept the illusion of being an observer.

SCENES in fiction bring the action and sometimes the dialogue of the characters before the reader with a fullness comparable to what a witness might observe or overhear if he had been present. Usually the scenic parts of a fictional work can be located by flipping casually through the pages until the eye catches the marks indicating dialogue.

Although scenes bring to the reader an amplitude of detail comparable to that of reality, a moment's reflection tells us that comparison can only reveal an illusion. Prose simply cannot catalogue all the details that would be recorded by a movie camera. It can, however, select and emphasize a crucial pattern of detail as no camera ever could.

The composition of a short story is a constant juggling act, with the author trying always to give the effect of fully reported scenes while still keeping them as brief as possible. The stories in this volume show various ingenious compromises between fullness and economy, and none of them represents perfection. A scene is, by its nature, a compromise, and it is illogical to call any compromise perfect.

But indeed there can be splendid compromises. A very considera ble part of the aesthetic pleasure we get from reading fiction comes from appreciation of the virtuosity evident in the design of scenes.

Stories that open with scenes have some definite advantages over those opening with narrative or description. They immediately catch the reader's interest by the direct encounter of characters and the sensuous detail of movement. They have the corresponding disadvantage—the reader has not been prepared to see what is significant in the profusion of scenic detail. An opening scene can bewilder the unprepared reader and set up expectations that the story will not fulfill.

This risk is not ordinarily a grave one. What is not fully clarified in the opening passages of fiction will normally be made to disclose its meaning by what follows. Every reader knows a story can't be blurted out as instantaneous revelation. If you have roused his interest by a dramatic opening, he is usually content to read on and see what the encounter meant.

Of the stories in this book, "The Best of Everything" and "Murphy's Xmas" begin scenically. The latter moves directly ahead from this initial scene, building its complex and poignant web by a series of allusions to Murphy's extramarital involvements and other quandaries that have brought him to his present passion. It should also be pointed out that, though the story is a self-contained unit, it is also the terminal story in a book of stories *(The Murphy Stories)*, all having to do with Murphy's entanglements.

The scene that opens "The Best of Everything" turns out to be the middle of the story the author will unfold. The day before Grace's wedding is not the beginning of her involvement with Ralph—that beginning will be told in a flashback after the scene has established the characters—but it is the start of a present, unified action that will terminate with his visit to her apartment. This story is a good example of the kind that begins "in the middle of things." It is worth studying for its fine scenic construction and for the smooth, deft use of a flashback.

Note well that while the flashback represents a movement backward in time, it actually advances our knowledge of the characters introduced in the preceding scene. It comes in at just the moment necessary to answer some of the questions presented by the scene. (Why is Grace going to marry a man so different from herself, a man whom, in her terms, she hardly even knows?)

The story illustrates another cardinal principle of using flashbacks: Make sure that something has been developed in the present scene to waken the interest of the reader. Create some degree of suspense before you move back into the past. Nothing is as out of place as a flashback stuck into a story before the reader knows why he ought to care about what happened before.

Sometimes a short story consists of a single scene, resembling a one act play. There are several fine Hemingway stories of this kind, and since you owe it to yourself to know the work of this modern master very well, I recommend that you read his collected stories for the way they reveal character and economically yield the meaning of the action.

More commonly, though, a series of scenes—however brief—is required to expose the complication and evolution so necessary to fiction. Nothing is more crucial or demanding than choosing those parts of the story-in-your-head that require or permit full scenic development. To shape my story "In the Central Blue," it seemed obvious that the actual trip made by the youngsters to see the movie had to be rendered in a group of closely connected scenes. The choice of including the earlier scene in which the narrator quarrels with his friend Hudson is difficult to justify except in nebulous terms of my feeling about the balance, pace, intensity and tone of the story. That earlier scene *feels* right to me.

The purpose of a scene at, or very near, the end of a story is to provide an occasion for the showdown between whatever forces have been in conflict through the body of the action. Such a showdown scene is sometimes referred to—in fiction as well as in the drama—as an "obligatory scene." It is obligatory in the sense that when one fighter says he can lick another he must stage a test encounter to see if he is right. Another example might be found in the conventional Western story where the rustler claims he can beat the sheriff to the draw. They have to shoot it out to determine which is faster. A scene permits the reader some degree of illusion that he is present when the showdown comes.

Is it necessary to end stories with an obligatory scene—with a dramatic resolution the reader has been led to expect? There is no final answer. Many fine stories are concluded with such scenes. Some are not. The principle that must be respected is that every story must have *some* resolution, some denouement, whether this is accomplished scenically or otherwise. Chekhov said once that if, in the opening passages of a story, the author mentions a gun hanging over a mantelpiece, the story isn't properly finished until that gun has been fired. A climactic, obligatory scene obviously offers a good chance for someone to shoot it off.

It might be useful to you to compare the number of scenes, their length, and their relation to linking passages of narrative in each of the stories in this book. You'll find that the structure is different in each. Each one was built according to the requirements of the subject. There is no such thing as an ideal mechanical form that could be imposed with equal propriety on such different kinds of material.

Note that there is also variety among the scenes of any one of the stories. Not all are the same length. Not all of them are intended to focus the reader's interest on the same sorts of things.

A HALF-SCENE is essentially an integral part of a narrative passage. It is an interruption of pace, not a shift to another kind of presentation. It is not intended to be complete in itself. It is clearly subordinate in significance to the passage of narrative in which it is placed. It might be thought of as mere relief to the eye of the reader, tired from a prolonged passage of narrative.

But it is more than that. It is a momentary shift from a distant view of the subject to a close-up, not designed to present a dramatic resolution but to borrow some of the qualities of the scene for a sample—as if to show what the narrative is really talking about.

A great deal of Chekhov's fiction is scenic in quality, even when true scenes are used sparsely. His wonderful long story "My Life" offers such a dexterous use of half-scenes that one almost imagines himself to be reading a series of scenes from one of Chekhov's plays. Actually, narrative makes up the bulk of many sections of the story.

From "The Lady with the Pet Dog" I'll extract one example for illustration. In Section III of that story there is narrative exposition of Gurov's desire to share his memories of Anna with someone. In the very midst of this exposition comes the transition into scenic presentation.

Gurov says to an official with whom he had been playing cards:

"If you only knew what a fascinating woman I became acquainted with at Yalta!"

The official got into his sledge and was driving away, but turned suddenly and shouted:

"Dmitry Dmitrich!"

"What is it?"

"You were right this evening: the sturgeon was a bit high."

That's all we're given of this encounter between two men, and we realize that in and by itself it has not accomplished the things we expect of a scene. The narrative resumes immediately to explain Gurov's indignation at the general crassness around him which frustrates even his wish to share memories. The narrative tells us more than the inserted dialogue shows us. But the little exchange has given us a sudden, stunning insight into what the narrative is actually referring to. It's a sample set in to throw its ugly light on the whole complex period covered by the narration.

A half-scene will not do the job that scenes can do in advancing the story line or permitting characters to reveal themselves. But properly handled, it will lend some of the emotional directness and liveliness of scene to extended passages of narrative.

DIALOGUE is a fundamental ingredient of most scenes or half-scenes. Beyond this, we ought to recognize that it is such a useful technical resource it deserves study and practice in its own right.

More than anything else, perhaps, good dialogue brings a sense of life to fiction—of life precisely observed and candidly recreated. The great fictional requirement of concreteness is satisfied by dialogue as by few other resources at a writer's command, because the reader is permitted to hear the characters of a story speaking in their own voices, revealing the most delicate shades of personality and interest by what they say or ask.

Poor dialogue, on the other hand, gives away the writer's ineptitude more quickly and more devastatingly than any other fumbled passages of his story. He can tell us that his chief female character is witty, lively, and cheerful. And we are likely to believe him, up to a point. But if the girl then speaks like a stupid, conventional sourpuss, no amount of persuasion by the author will convince the canny reader that she is anything else.

Our first demand on dialogue, then, is that it should conform to character and be natural. (Even in a fantasy or other highly artificial kinds of fiction this simple principle will hold. If characters speak in fantastic situations and fantastic environments, their speech ought to sound native to such situations or settings.)

There is, alas, no way to teach anyone to write natural-sounding dialogue. Concentration in reading good dialogue will help—but only if one uses what he learns from reading as a guide to *listening* to the way people talk in real life. The fundamental truth remains: You must learn by listening.

More important than this (and easier, too), get the habit of listening to yourself. Naturalness in fictional dialogue requires that a single character should express himself differently according to the circumstance in which he finds himself. You don't sound the same when you crawl sleepily and anxiously out of bed in the morning as you will later in the day when your roommate pawns your typewriter. Whether you know it or not, you use a monstrous variety of voices in carrying on your everyday life. What do all these voices say?

Listening to yourself, learning your own voices, will pay off splendidly when you have to invent dialogue. In creating a scene you have to become something of an actor. Confronted with a particular situation, what would you say in the place of your character? If you know what you would naturally say in his predicament, you can probably approximate natural-sounding speech for him. Then you can tinker with the approximation like a piano tuner among the strings until you've given the speech its exact and proper note.

Ordinarily it is a mistake to try to reproduce dialect by phonetic spelling. And if you concentrate more on the peculiarities of a character's speech than on its common qualities, you are more apt to caricature him than to bring him alive. Only one story in this book—"The Best of Everything"—exploits the special speech patterns of its characters by distortions of spelling: " 'Whaddya—in a hurry a somethin?' " says Eddie. Ralph says, " 'Wha' happen ta you, wise guy?' " In this story there is probably a good reason for such a practice. The difference between Grace's sensibility and Ralph's—revealed by different manners of speech—adds poignancy to their mistake in thinking they can marry.

Nevertheless, such distortions ought to be used very sparingly, and when there is no overwhelming indication that they are needed, they are apt to annoy the reader more than they can enlighten him. Note that a great many of the effects Mr. Yates achieves in his dialogue come from imitating the vocabulary and syntax of Ralph and Eddie rather than from phonetic spelling. " 'Ah, you don't want the roommate, Eddie. The roommate's a dog. A snob, too, I think. No but this *other* one, this little *Gracie*—boy, I mean, she is *stacked.*' "

We recognize this as Ralph's true and natural voice, though every syllable is spelled correctly.

In building passages of dialogue, remember that any statement or question may draw a variety of responses. Frequently an indirect response gives a more natural effect than a direct one.

Suppose, for instance, that one character addresses another in this fashion: "Is your girdle too tight?"

The direct answer would be "Yes," "No," or "Not really."

But how much more lifelike if the lady so addressed responds, "Let me out of here! Stop the elevator! Let me out of here!"

Even better, she might answer, "I was on my way to shop for a spring suit."

The indirect response is often better because it conforms to the fact that dialogues in actual life are often two or more interrupted monologues. Two minds are seldom operating on the same wave length. Therefore the answer that A has in mind when he asks a question is not always the answer that B is stimulated to give.

In the last example above, it would seem that the lady questioned is merely reminded, by the question, of her reason for putting on the tight girdle in the first place. Her mind is shown spinning on its own orbit, merely tangential to that of the questioner. And so it often is in reality.

As a rule of thumb, we might say that direct response in dialogue is more appropriate when the objective situation fuses the interest of the speakers.

So, when a lion is approaching and one hunter says to another, "Is your gun loaded?" the second would, in all probability, say "Yes" or "No."

Indirect response reveals the mental gulf between speakers when each is busier with his own thoughts than with the superficial subject of the conversation.

Two men are having drinks before catching a train for home. One says, "My boss was on the warpath today." The other replies, "I forgot to buy the birdseed Beulah asked me to bring."

Modulation from the direct to the indirect and back is a means of control over passages of dialogue. It permits a range of exposure extending from the purely superficial to the profound.

Dialogue serves a definite, though limited, purpose in providing a change of pace in extended passages of narration. The reader's eye welcomes the novelty in lines set off by quotation marks.

Also, when one speaker has a great deal to say—several paragraphs of information, perhaps—the interspersal of comments from the persons listening to him will serve as a reminder that they are still on the scene.

These usages are of no great importance. They are no more than mechanical practices. But, of course, the careful writer will concern himself with every aspect of his work. He will always remember that the mechanics of fiction are among the resources with which he must work his magic.

4

FINGER EXERCISES

The teacher of writing knows that sometimes the most promising young writers are frustrated to the point of rage and brought to a standstill by the discrepancy between their intentions (which are clear enough to them) and their performance in writing (whose shortcomings are just as clear). That is the time when orthodox *and* unorthodox suggestions are called for to get the stalled talent in motion again.

In most of the other chapters of this book the suggestions and advice are roughly orthodox. I have the feeling that the "finger exercises" I have to recommend here may be a little suspect to the true believers in the art of writing. But against that I lay my stout conviction that they can sometimes help.

I don't want you to keep butting your head against the stone wall of technical problems that are beyond your present means to solve. I'll admire anyone who does that—and gets groggily to his feet, lowers his bloody head, and runs again. But I know there's a law of diminishing returns in such blind gallantry. I have a notion that there may be exercises which, sometimes, may point a way around or over the wall.

But before describing some exercises that can be helpful, let me state one thing clearly: Whatever is produced as an exercise has no value in itself. It is a means to a desirable end. That is all.

Absolutely all. Your waste basket is the right and proper destination for everything you turn out as an exercise.

Now the exercises.

First, since the last chapter involved you in thinking about descriptions, bits of narration, and scenes, it seems that it might be useful to write a number of each of these story fragments.

Practice short, medium, and long descriptions. Remember that the grand objective in any description is to distinguish a particular and concrete thing from all that resembles it. When Flaubert was coaching young de Maupassant, he told him to go watch the cab drivers in front of a Parisian railway station and practice describing *one* of them in language that would single him out from all the rest hanging around there.

Obviously more than the use of language is involved in such practice. It is also an exercise in observation, in the selection of significant details from the multitude of common ones. (All French cab drivers have red noses and greedy eyes—but *only one* sits in his cab with the peculiar poise of a man driving a racing sulky at a provincial fair.)

In practicing fragments of narrative, the observation of striking particulars won't help much. It is not the nature of narrative to depend greatly on detail. Rather, in such exercises you ought to test your power to generalize and summarize an extensive action or period of time.

"After six tedious months of training at Camp Vandiver, my regiment embarked from San Francisco. . . ." And then? What was the quality and general content of the next six months? Of the month after that? And the following week? And of the morning just before the adjutant stabbed the Colonel?

Answer the general questions following from some such statement as I gave in quotes, and you have a narrative passage. All you need now is a story in which to use it . . . No? Try another practice shot. Another. Everything you put on paper—if you do it conscientiously—helps you get the feel of the medium in which you have chosen to work. Write *something* every day, even if it must remain a homeless fragment, doomed to the waste basket. Write it as well as you possibly can.

In practicing scenes it may be good training for you to go from some scene in your daily, normal life straight to your writing desk and (1) put down *everything* you can remember of the setting, the appearance of the people in it, their actions, and their dialogue; or (2) try to make an economical selection from all you remember and form it so that it will convey the essential quality of the scene as you felt it.

Again, in such practice, you are testing your powers of observation and recall. The more you demand of them, the more valuable the exercise.

But remember—when you're getting pretty cocky about your capacity to hold a great deal in a photographic memory—that a writer doesn't and shouldn't observe in the same way a camera or tape recorder would. As a general principle it is better to observe as a participant than as a bystander. Even though the participant in a scene misses some detail that a bystander might note, active, wholehearted participation requires that the emotions work automatically to select what counts from the noise that doesn't. For purposes of practice in writing scenes it is probably better to write of an occasion when you've quarreled with your girl than of one in which you have, from the sidelines, watched a crueler man beat *his* girl with a chair leg and then defy the police who came after him.

I know a writer who talks a lot—in fact, shouts a lot—at parties, and yet he has the uncanny ability to hear, over the sound of his own voice, all that really characterizes the commotion around him. He may be socially boorish, but as a writer he knows what he's doing. I guess he's using his loud voice as a kind of screen to keep insignificant detail out of his consciousness—and to draw unguarded responses from those he tempts into argument with him.

I also want to propose some exercises of imitation. That word—*imitation*—will sound simply horrid to many writers and to the very best of the inexperienced ones. What? you'll say. Imitation? If I can't at least be original, then writing is a pure waste of my time. Besides, it isn't fair to copy someone else. . . .

Now of course it is cheating to imitate anyone else's work and try to pass the result off as your own contribution to literature. Who said you should try to pass it anywhere except into the incinerator?

To anyone who truly fears that a little indoor imitation will set him in a rut he can't break out of, or set his foot on a path that will lead inevitably to embezzlement and counterfeiting U.S. currency, I must say, for heaven's sake, don't do it. But I strongly believe that those with enough equanimity to try a few imitations now and then will learn something about their craft that can hardly be learned so quickly in any other way. It is only to them that the following comments are addressed.

By now you have read the short stories in this book at least once and have, I hope, returned to them either for rereading or for examination of certain special elements in them. They offer a very large body of material from which you might select, for imitation, passages that have particularly impressed you.

Let me simply show, by imitating the first three paragraphs of "The Best of Everything," how you should go about it:

> Some of his friends thought George might go on a rampage the day after his wife left him. As a precaution, two of them stayed overnight at his house, though he had not asked for company.
>
> A crumpled note lay among the unwashed plates on the kitchen table—from Miranda, his wife—and the three short sentences in Miranda's careful script explained sufficiently why she had gone home to Monterey. Miranda had considered their marriage a hollow mockery since she found out about the girl in the beach house at Carmel, and yesterday when she confronted him in tears, he had turned his back on her, busying himself with some unnecessary repair work, whistling and refusing to answer her accusations.
>
> "Got to get this rain gutter mended, Miranda," he had said. "Bad weather coming. Why don't you go shopping and forget about *that?*"

Now, with the text open beside you for reference, write your own imitation in three exactly parallel paragraphs. If such an exercise has no other value, it will absolutely force you to concentrate on *what there is in Mr. Yates's paragraphs that has to be imitated.*

You have to imitate the number of sentences and their relative length and complexity, their grammatic structure.

You have to imitate detail that characterizes scene and actors.
You have to imitate the point of view.

You have to imitate the use of proper names and pronouns.

You have to imitate the emotional state of the characters that gives them their relationship in the scene.

In a word, you cannot do this sort of imitation without thinking pretty nimbly about what you are doing. You are performing one of the kinds of thought that is part of original composition, and if the example you are imitating serves as a kind of crutch, it also serves as a test of your power to shape the material of your own imagination to a predetermined form.

If I have begun by advocating a rather dry and mechanical form of imitation, let me conclude by saying that imitation shades very gradually into all works that we properly think of as original. There cannot be, and probably there should never be, any piece of fiction that does not derive from other literary works, though the connections between one piece and whatever served as a model may be infinitely subtle and varied.

As a writer continues the practice of his art he will find more subtle and varied ways of drawing on what has already been done. Long after he stops getting any good from the simple kinds of imitation I have described, a writer may have evolved his own fashion of drawing on someone else's style or imagination. He may quite deliberately choose a theme or a mannerism that "belongs" to someone else with the intention of working his own variations on it. In such case he does not at all want to hide the source of his borrowing, but rather hopes it will be obvious to the reader.

In my own case I have found for some years that it helps me get started to work in the morning if I pull out a book and read a little bit—two or three paragraphs or a couple of stanzas of poetry. It doesn't matter, apparently, whether what I read has any overt connection with the thing I'm working on. All that matters is that what I read should be good enough to catch my own verbal imagination and drag it until it begins to move under its own power. Perhaps this reliance on an assist in taking off should not be categorized as imitation at all, and yet I have the idea that it may be at least an imitation of the creative drive my intuition finds in what I have read. And certainly it fulfills the one function that can be claimed for imitation—that of giving impetus and direction when the writer finds himself at a halt.

There is another practice that might be called either an exercise or a phase of composition—depending on what results are achieved by it. At any rate, it is experimental in nature and very often gives no rewards except a broader, clearer notion of the possibilities among which a writer may choose in presenting his story.

This might be given the general name *conversion*. It is vaguely comparable to transposing a piece of music from one key to another. If, for example, a story has been written in the first person ("I went home to Denmark after my father's death"), it can be a rewarding experiment to try the same story in the third person: ("After his father's death, Hamlet went home to Denmark.")

You might try such conversion on one of the stories in this book, but since it involves so much labor, you might well choose to try it instead on a story of your own, in the hope that a different manner of narration might give it a fresh start.

But before you begin your own revision, consider what changes would have to be made in some of these stories if the person of the narration were changed.

If you substituted the pronoun "I" for the name "Grace" in "The Best of Everything," the first several paragraphs might need no major alteration. It is perfectly plausible that someone might be reporting her own day at the office just before she is to be married in the same objective terms the author has used. But when we come to the flashback describing the courtship that has preceded the present scene there would be a real necessity for the narrator to justify her choice of Ralph as a husband. The sleepwalking inertia that seems, in the present version, to be carrying her helplessly into this marriage would not be acceptable at all if it were offered as explanation by a girl explaining her own case. (This is probably a sufficient reason for leaving Yates's story as it is. We need go no further with our imaginary conversion than is required to show what alterations would have to be made if the manner of narration were changed.)

Of course there are more ways of converting—or recasting—stories than by shifting the person of the narration.

For practice in revision you might try converting a grim and bleak story into comedy.

Try making fantasy from realism and realism from fantasy.

Try converting a story told mostly in author's prose into one made up mostly of dramatic dialogue.

Cut a story up into its separate paragraphs. (Yes, with scissors.) Make a new arrangement of paragraphs, write whatever connective passages are necessary to make the new arrangement coherent, and paste the result together to make a new manuscript. Does this strike you as being akin to cutting out paper dolls? It isn't, and even if it were it could help you convince yourself that a work of fiction is a plastic thing that *may* be rearranged into innumerable forms. When you realize that fully, you'll handle your own work with more freedom and authority. You'll stop being bossed by the qualities in it that are merely accidental.

Try reducing a story to half its length without losing essential meaning. In the same spirit, build one up by adding scenes where narrative passages served before.

Try replacing all proper nouns with pronouns in a story. This experiment will call for an adjustment of modifiers to keep identities separate and distinct. It is from the adjustments that you learn.

Enough. I have suggested exercises and experiments in revision that could keep anyone busy for a long time—and keep him from doing the new stories he should be writing.

5

NOTEBOOKS
AND LISTS

It should go without saying that fiction writers keep notebooks. They may also keep files where fragmentary bits and unfinished manuscripts are systematically saved, along with stories due for revision and tear sheets from various publications that may come in handy someday.

But notebooks are not just portable filing systems—or, at least, they should not be. They ought to be *work* books where the entries are constantly amended, developed, and put in new combinations. They are, for the writer, what sketchbooks are to the painter—a place to begin and continue the labors of composition before one is quite sure what stories may emerge from the compositional process.

Coming across material and retrieving it in verbal form for your notebook is an act of the imagination—an incompleted act without the subsequent labors of combining your discoveries into a unified form, but one of the most crucial steps in assuring that your fiction will have the throb of life. Gather into your notebook the concrete data of colors, shapes, names, and the way things work. Seize the overheard lines of dialogue that characterize and evoke the essence of a person, a situation, a time, a place, a moral climate. Sift incidents from the evening news, from gossip. (How many of the tales of Henry James grew from the germs of ideas picked up as anecdotes in dinner conversation!) Enter the words and phrases that seem to rise of themselves from the stimuli of nature, play, parties, ceremonies, and manual labor. In *Ulysses* the young writer, Stephen Dedalus, walking on the beach, draws forth from his verbal savings account the phrase, "a day of dappled, sea-borne clouds." Accumulate a list of such phrases to match the days when the weather you walk in somehow matches the weather of memory and feeling.

Only—be sure that what you put into your notebooks really has grabbed your imagination. Don't let your notebooks (or your filing system, for that matter) turn into wastebaskets glutted with indifferent and inert trash of merely "interesting" or titillating appeal. As a rule of thumb we might say that whatever seems as striking as part of a dream surely must be entered—stuff that seems to be simultaneously familiar and strange. And for that matter, a journal of your actual dreams might well be interspersed with your other gleanings.

Writers work *from* their notebooks when they begin or when they flesh out their stories. The stuff that has been sifted into a notebook is already half fictionalized. But it is more important to realize that writers also work *in* their notebooks, constantly shifting and combining, reviewing and recombining what their observant senses have found. They are constantly asking, "What goes with what?"— as they recopy and repaste material until, sometimes, a major new idea springs from a lucky combination of items gathered from an unplanned variety of sources. ("Unplanned"?—the lower levels of your consciousness plan more honestly than the upper levels; that is why dreams are so trustworthy when one has learned to interpret them well.)

Perhaps it will help to think of your notebooks as incubators. The fertile, isolated entry you made on Tuesday may be an intuition of some crucial theme you are not yet ready to contemplate in its entirety. Perhaps you have not yet seen enough of the world to make it fully comprehensible. Save it and wait. Have faith that what seemed initially a single glimmer may, in the course of your further work, be part of a continuous series of illuminations.

Many writers have left us notebooks that are at least comparable in merit to their more formal publications. I have particularly cherished those of Chekhov, Hawthorne, and Virginia Woolf. Take a look at one of these if you want a model. Cyril Connolly's best book, by far, is a sort of notebook—*The Unquiet Grave*. It is lovingly, scrupulously cultivated and polished so that every entry enriches and is enriched by all the others. And W. H. Auden's *A Certain World* is another example that falls within my definition of a writer's notebook. He calls it a "commonplace book." It contains his gleanings from many years of reading. By whatever name, it is a shining revelation of the poet's imagination in play—in the play of discovery—and that is what you must try to make of your notebook.

A writer's life is a long training in observation and in his notebook the material of observation undergoes part of its transformation into the syntax of sentences, the shapes of paragraphs and the larger units of finished composition. It is natural enough that at some stage of the transformation the material should appear in the form of lists. Lists are a sort of presyntactical ordering and clustering of things caught up in the net of our concerns. Emerson told us that "bare" lists of words are enough to set off the imagination and control its direction. You can prove the truth of this easily by making lists of people who have frightened you, of sensations that induce sleepiness, or of words you associate with war.

See? A story begins to form around the items in the list—and if you continue the experiment by changing the sequence of items, you will see that the ghostly story begins to change in quality. If you were to explain in detail what the separate items in your list had to do with each other, you would be going one step farther in storytelling.

To increase your awareness of how "bare" lists continue to function according to their qualities and sequence when they are incorporated in the finished syntax of prose, jot down the list of nouns or verbs you find on any page of any story in this book and read it over a day after you have read the story, noting the way in which your imagination is stimulated and controlled. Remember that many of the poems of Walt Whitman owe their majesty to the fact that they are essentially lists—catalogings—of the occupations, delights, anxieties, memories, origins, creeds, and triumphs of the

Americans he celebrated *en masse* and as individuals. The lists in *Ulysses* provide endlessly varied comic effects as Joyce piles them up to the point of absurdity and tunes them with surprising shifts from realism to improbability. Vladimir Nabokov said—and you'd better believe him—that the part of *Lolita* which gave him the most satisfaction was the *list of the names* of Lolita's classmates.

To get you started with the assembling and manipulating of lists for your own writer's notebook, let me illustrate how three lists of concrete elements provide much of the organic substructure of my story "In the Central Blue." Note that each list has a flavor of its own, while there is some variation in flavor of the elements in each list. As you reflect on the finished story, you will realize that it is the interplay of these three clusters of reality that provides the conflict of emotions in the central character.

List I
Wings (a movie first released about 1930)
spring thaws
gravel road
model airplanes
grain elevator
Steven's Crackshot (a cheap, singleshot .22 rifle)
titless cousin
Essex (an automobile no longer manufactured)
moon-glinting railroad tracks
mother's perfume
War Aces (a magazine)
spatsies (a slang term for sparrows)

The list suggests the observable life of a boy in a rural community of the 1930s. Some of the elements faintly suggest the quality of his imaginative life—it is impossible to make any list of things in his environment that would not—but yet, by and large, these are the mundane exterior trappings of his existence. The list might have been jotted down by a very detached observer who knew and cared little about the boy's passions or fantasies.

List II
Luger
fuselage

Zeppelin
London
spring offensive
Lt. Frank Luke
negligee
Spad
Krauts
flight leader
Sam Browne belt

By itself, this list is a suggestive sampling of the actual historic circumstances of World War I. There really was a Lt. Frank Luke, an American aviator famed as "the Balloon–buster." German Zeppelins raided London and dropped bombs on that city. The macrocosm of history exists as part of the environment within which the boy in the story has to define himself and live. And yet, of course, historic reality comes to the boy, as it comes to most of us most of the time, by reports which are not easy to distinguish from fantasy. These reports are transformed into fantasy by such popular entertainments as the movie *Hell's Angels*, which figures so importantly in the story.

How did the word *negligee* get into this list so obviously dominated by masculine and military concerns? I put it there, as I put it into the story—so that its erotic and nostalgic connotations would startle and amuse you *because* it is "out of place." It is the teaser in the list. In the movie, worn by Jean Harlow, it was the teaser.

List III
tickles
kisses
silks
cleavage
"doing intercourse"
ravish
buttons
quick feel
Silver Screen (magazine)
hot breath

This third list is evidently unified by its exclusive concentration on the erotic concerns of a boy in his early teens. As you see from reading the story, there is a hopeless confusion among these elements in his mind. He can't reasonably distinguish between the promise of Jean Harlow's cleavage, proffered by the movie and the movie magazine, and the flat bosom of young Betty Carnahan. He isn't sure just what sort of ravishment he might be capable of in any event. What he can lay hands on is altogether incommensurate with the magnitude of yearning that has been stirred up inside him by the incitements of his world.

The story I wrote is not quite "all there" in these three lists. But hopefully the dynamics of conflict that make it exist as a story are more readily discernible when these concrete elements are separated from the syntax and the voice of the narrator.

Actually, I did not set down these lists in my notebook before I wrote this particular story. But I might have. The story might have come more easily if I had. And I am convinced that in my mind as I wrote, or before I wrote, the lists were present. Insofar as I can understand my own compositional processes, I'd say that some sort of clustering of elements (which is the same thing as listing) always precedes any actual writing.

Therefore my recommendation follows with inevitable logic: Make lists as a preparation for writing. Experiment in your notebook by changing the order of elements in your lists, adding items that may at first seem incongruous, for the sake of surprise and irony. Draw on your memory. Draw on immediate observation. Draw on such sources of information as reading, lectures, television.

Set two or three lists in arbitrary combination on a single page. What stirring of your imagination toward a story begins when you note possible conflicts or harmonies among these words that you have forced into proximity without any preconceived plan?

Perhaps the true value of this exercise is to thwart preconceptions and permit the emergence into consciousness of things we didn't know we knew. For surely much of our capacity for observation is inhibited by rigidities of expectation. We report what we are trained to report—until we invent capricious ways to ease ourselves out of our blinders.

I have sometimes asked students to make, and then combine, (1) a list of verbs that pertain to eating a meal, (2) a list of adjectives descriptive of their classmates, and (3) a list of well-loved places. Arbitrarily or on inspiration they string verb-adjective-noun combinations from these juxtaposed lists after the subject pronoun *I.*

Examples:
> *I savor elfin Portsmouth.*
> *I salt intemperate Bristol.*
> *I sip lazy Vermont.*

Perhaps these examples seem merely freakish to anyone reading them cold. But surely they are better than: *I enjoyed picturesque Vermont.* And for the student who made them according to the playful method of shuffling lists together they may draw after them strings of suggestion attached to chunks of remembered observation that will enliven all the language that precedes and follows when they are socked into a paragraph.

All word games, like this one, are potentially valuable to the writer willing to play them with zest. No doubt a fondness for such verbal sport is one of the earliest and surest symptoms of literary promise. And sometimes from the random combinations thus produced will come glimmering hints of the bedrock analogies that link all our responses of preference, action, and interpretation. Metaphors both natural and fresh may rise to the level of consciousness in the midst of sport. Words will seem to choose themselves, and in matters of diction there is nothing better than that.

The search for the right word that honestly represents our best and fullest perceptions will, of course, go beyond the sometimes arbitrary results of verbal gamesmanship. The delight one takes in all inventive variations is very important in advancing the search.

SECTION TWO

THE STORIES

R. V. CASSILL

IN THE
CENTRAL BLUE

This is an example of first-person narration. *In some very loose, general way the story conforms to things that happened to me as a boy, to feelings I once knew, and to an amusement I felt in recalling their useless pain. But . . . I was completely ruthless in adapting things remembered to the requirements of fiction. Therefore it is proper for me to refer to the person telling the story as a character I have created.*

The story opens with expository narrative. *Thereafter, as much as possible is rendered* dramatically, *with an overlay of comment by the narrator to sustain the* voice *of the mature person recollecting a childhood event.*

The setting *of the story—a rural community during the Depression—works to highlight the ironic discrepancy between the boy's wishes and the reality he must inhabit. This discrepancy provides the basic* conflict.

The climax *of the story—and it is deliberately* understated—*occurs when the boy calls his father a bastard and the father declines to strike him for his impudence. "I saw him in his human dimension," he says. An insight has been won at the cost of humiliation and grief.*

Ordinarily I considered it no drawback that there was no theater in our little farming town of Chesterfield. But in the case of World War I air movies I felt different. At puberty I was very airminded, and it seemed a large disaster when I missed *Wings*.

The week it played in Nebraska City spring thaws took the

"In the Central Blue" originally appeared in *Man and the Movies*, W. R. Robinson, ed. (Baton Rouge: Louisiana State University Press, 1967).

bottom out of the gravel road for miles east of the bridge we would have to cross to get there. Toward the end of the week when the road began to get firmer, I was struck down by fever and diarrhea. My affliction was probably brought on by anxiety about the road conditions and by arguing with my father about whether, at full power and with three boys to push, his Essex might not churn its way through the bad spots to the bridge.

My older brother and my best friend Hudson Fowler saw the picture, driving over to Nebraska City at the week's end with a truck full of other kids from Chesterfield. From an upstairs window I watched the truck pull away, crouched in my weakness, nursing the envy manifested in the uncontrollable, spastic burning of my gut. My father hunted me out to say that if I "had taken care of myself"—instead of dashing across wet lawns and fields outside of town all week without boots to prove that the earth was *not* mirey underfoot—I might now be going with the others. If I just hadn't got so excited about a darn airplane movie, I wouldn't have overtaxed my system.

The lesson was plain enough without his pointing the moral. But I wouldn't have it. In the darkness of the privy that evening I shit it away. In their wobbly, sassy little Spads, the boys had gone up there without me. The little line of dots pocked the canvas of their fuselages. Spitting black blood, their clean American faces lolled on the padded rims of the cockpits. In his black triplane with a black scarf crackling in the slipstream, the Kraut laughed at us all. Wind whistled around the ill–fitting privy door. Its mockery and the stink of my own excrement were no more offensive to me than my father's common sense judgment on my psychosomatic folly. I rebelled against them all.

So, if I had missed *Wings*, I was not going to miss *Hell's Angels*. After so long a time, I'm not sure how much later, it came to the theater in Nebraska City. It must have come at least a year afterward, because by then both my friend Hudson and I had graduated into high school, my older brother got to take the car out in the evening for dates, and I was in love with Hudson's blonde and titless cousin Betty.

I loved her ignorantly, impurely, and intermittently, sometimes unfurling toward her passions that had been cultivated for other objects and which were, no doubt, more appropriate when directed toward building model airplanes, shooting Germanic spatsies from the mulberry tree with antiaircraft fire from my Stevens' Crackshot, or working up nurse-aviator fantasies by a near simultaneous reading of *War Aces* and *Silver Screen* magazines.

Good little Betty couldn't have known what I wanted of her when I scrimmaged for a seat next to her in algebra class. At Halloween of our freshman year I caught her by accident as she was coming—costumed and masked—across the parking lot to the back entrance of the high school building to the party. She couldn't have known what I did to her then when I drew her out of the moonlight into the shadow of the fire escape and kissed her. I took off running in the direction of the Chesterfield grain elevator and went past it for a mile down the moon-glinting railroad tracks, convinced that I had done to her what Lieutenant Frank Luke did to the French nurse before he took off for his last spree of balloon busting.

So she couldn't have known what I had in store for her when I invited her to go to Nebraska City with me to see *Hell's Angels*. That is, she couldn't have guessed at thirteen—or at thirty-five for that matter, when she had boys of her own to study and wonder about—what role she had been assigned to play in my intense imaginative life. She might have expected that I would try to kiss her in the car while we were riding home from Nebraska City with my brother and his date after the movie was over. Certainly I meant to do that and probably try to put one of my hands where she would eventually have breasts like Jean Harlow's. At thirteen she was prepared to sink her nails in my impudent hand and laugh it off with a merry, "None of *that!*"

But it was not a physical assault on her that I planned or needed. I was going to ravish her mind. With the aid of this powerful movie plus a few tickles and kisses afterward, I was going to wheedle her mind right away into the realm of wish and nonsense, where I was so lonely all by myself.

I had been making myself at home there since I had first begun to understand what this movie was going to be about. Of course I hadn't seen it yet, but months before I had read about it—probably in *Silver Screen*—and seen pictures of Jean Harlow in white furs with those big, bruise-toned spots under her eyes, of the burning Zeppelin, and of the Sam Browne-belted heroes who tangled with both.

There had been a bit of verse in the piece I read:

> *Hell's angels,*
> *Soaring in the central blue,*
> *As though to conquer Heaven*
> *And plant the banner of Lucifer*
> *On the most high. . . .*

It was the verse which provided the cipher or incantation that really took me out. Out *there*. Through the hot days of that summer there would be a lot of occasions when I was lying there with my bare naked thigh against the chill linoleum, beating away with the Harlow picture propped up in front of me, and just before I came, in that instant of focused self-awareness when I had stopped listening for the sound of my mother moving in the kitchen or my father or brother entering the house, I would say "In the central blue" and *be there*. I would be one of them. And I thought, wouldn't it be a lot happier if Betty would become one too and be out there with me, since she was a girl?

What? Beg pardon? Once again . . . ? How did I think this mating in the central blue was going to take place?

No use asking. I am no longer a mystic, so I no longer know. I repeat, merely, that in those months before my fourteenth birthday I anticipated that with the help of *Hell's Angels* I was going to ravish Betty Carnahan's mind. Too bad that I can't give a more satisfactory explanation. Anyway, it was in the hope of mental ravishment that I made the date with her two weeks before the movie came and with breathless stealth arranged that the two of us would go over to Nebraska City with my brother and his girl to see it.

Hudson Fowler behaved despicably when he heard that I was taking Betty. He acted as if it was his right to go with me if I had found a ride. "Get your mind above your belt," he said. "What do you want to do intercourse with that little nitwit for?"

"I don't," I said. I was shocked on many counts. Shocked by so much resentment from him just because I wasn't asking him along. His odd choice of expression shocked me into awareness that there was a fishy unreality in my plans for Betty.

He saw he had me on the defensive. "You pretend you're just interested in the airplanes," he crowed.

"They're burning a two-million-dollar zeppelin in this one."

"While all the time you just want an excuse to see Jean Harlow's legs. Listen, I've got a notion to show Aunt Ellen that dirty magazine you gave me and see if she lets Betty go with you at all."

The dirty magazine he alluded to was my copy of the movie magazine with choice shots of Miss Harlow in her starring role. It could hardly have shocked Mrs. Carnahan into an interference with my date. Hudson, with unscrupulous insight into the uses I had put it to, was merely using it to discomfort me.

"All right. Go ahead and take her," he said savagely. "But just remember this. Whatever happens over there"—he made *over there* sound splendidly more like Flanders Fields than like Nebraska City—"I've already done intercourse with her."

In the face of such challenge I had to claim, "Well, so have I."

"At the family reunion in Sidney. Behind the rodeo barns."

"At the Halloween party. On the school fire escape," I said.

Then we both called each other liars and backed away, throwing sticks and bits of bark and finally good sized rocks at each other's heads.

I should have known he wouldn't let it go at that. He got to my brother and with some sort of specious implication that I, his best friend, wouldn't dream of seeing this great movie without him, he arranged to go with us. Having conned my brother, Hudson insinuated to Betty and his Aunt Ellen that I hadn't so much been asking for a date as offering to share a historical cultural experience with Betty when I invited her to the movie. I suppose that such an implication was welcome to Mrs. Carnahan, in spite of my good reputation.

At any rate, when I bounded up on the Carnahan's porch just before dusk on that cold December afternoon—freshly bathed and shivering and wearing just a dash of my mother's perfume—who should come out in answer to my knock but Betty *and* Hudson. I didn't know then what arrangements had been made behind my back. All I knew was that I couldn't stand there, practically within earshot of Mrs. Carnahan and Betty's father, and go through the argument about Betty with Hudson again. He had me.

He had me good, and the rest of the evening was just one failing attempt after another to retrieve what I could from the disastrous misunderstandings he had set going. At least on the ride over Betty sat between Hudson and me in the back seat of the Essex. I fancied that she got a whiff or two of me in spite of the strong perfume she was wearing. Hudson and I bellowed the Air Force song back and forth for her benefit. In the front seat Betheen Hesseldahl, the big, cowy girl my brother was going with then, alternately nuzzled her face in his neck and sat as far away from him as she could move, asking for a cigarette. "Not in front of the kids," he growled. "Later," he promised. I managed to get my arm up on the back of the seat behind Betty for a mile or two. The trip over wasn't so bad.

But when we went into the theater things got horribly disarranged. I hung back politely to let the others slide into their seats first, and then found that Hudson was sitting between Betty and me. I could feel my bowels begin to writhe and burn. I leaned to Hudson's ear and called him a sonofabitch.

He caught me hard in the ribs with his elbow. "Ssssh! Look! There she is. Just like in the magazine."

What was going on—as I understood later, perhaps years later, when my equilibrium was at last restored—was the famous scene in which Harlow gets into something more comfortable. That was going on for the others. I was down between the rows of seats trying to get a lock on Hudson's arm and force him out of his place. He was trying to pay no attention to me. He burst into loud cackles, whether at the sight of Jean Harlow in *negligee* or at my plight I have no idea.

The usher came to quiet us. For the rest of the movie I huddled motionless. I wouldn't have trusted myself to try to speak, even at the break after the feature My brother sidled out past me to get popcorn for everyone and muttered, "What's the matter with you?" but I didn't answer him. Hudson said, "Boy, it really got me when that little plane came in over that big dirigible. You know it was *real.*" The sneak knew he had gone too far with me and was trying to make up, but I didn't even turn my head.

It was my impression that I didn't see a single bit of the movie. Only, afterward, as we were driving out of Nebraska City across that high, silvery bridge with the dry moon coming up over the Iowa bluffs, I began to get images that must have been before my eyes in the theater. Between the struts of the bridge I saw the RAF insignias and the snapping ribbons from the ailerons as the flight leader brought his planes up alongside us. There were black, darting shapes down where the silhouette of willows cut the reflecting glitter of ice near the Iowa shore.

A little later—not in any sequence that would have appeared in the film—I saw the Krauts in their zeppelin panic and prepare to cut loose the observation car dangling a mile below them over London. I was in that little teardrop contraption and I knew what they were doing. There was no way to stop them. Only a fool would have let himself in for such a mission.

And then Harlow was all over me. Her silks were jiggling like moonlight on my retinas and that white hair was moving in like a cloud on a high wind. The bruise-toned shadow of her cleavage was so close to my face that my eyes crossed trying to keep it in focus. I turned to Betty. She was leaning back quite peaceably in the crook of Hudson's shoulder. Her eyes were open and as far as I could make out, she was smiling. Hudson's free hand was stuck in between the buttons of her winter coat.

What I did then was inexcusable. That is, it is the kind of thing for which one's own psyche never, never finds a tolerable excuse, so that when you say to yourself long afterward, "Why I was only a fumbling, ignorant kid then," still the eye of memory averts itself.

While she leaned back in Hudson's arms, I tried to neck her. I tried to kiss her while his face was so close to hers that I could feel his hot breath on my cheek. I tried to unbutton her coat, not so much to get his hand out of it as to get mine in too.

"What are you little monkeys *doin'* back there?" Betheen Hessendahl wanted to know. She leaned over the back of the seat and giggled.

"You're crazy," Betty said.

"He's gone crazy," Hudson said, with maddening self-assurance. "Too much Harlow."

"Well, give everyone a cigarette," Betheen suggested.

My brother argued that the smell of tobacco would stay in the car and displease our parents. But in a minute he pulled to the side of the road and lit two. He gave one to Betheen and kept the other himself. After two drags she leaned back and passed it to us.

She passed it to Betty Carnahan, rather, and I can not describe the horror and excitement I felt when Betty leaned forward and puckered her lips to draw on it. It was not I who had had too much Harlow. It was Betty. Her mind had, somehow, been truly ravished by what she had seen. In the red glow from the cigarette a positively obscene merriment flickered over her little face. It was quite beyond anything I had meant for her. At that moment, and only then, I believed that she had been behind the rodeo barns at Sidney with her cousin.

I made up my mind then and there that after we had dropped Hudson at his house I would ask my brother to take Betty and me straight home. I knew it was his habit to take Betheen or one of his other girls to park down behind the grain elevator in an empty field at the end of his Sunday night dates, and in all the arrangements for this evening I thought it had been tacitly assumed that Betty and I might go there with them tonight. Now I didn't want to go. My mixed intentions had begun a process of depravity that had to be stopped. I wanted to go back to the innocence of that evening earlier in the fall when I had kissed Betty by the fire escape and run away.

Caught in such unfathomable hypocrisy, I hardly noticed that my brother stopped the car first in front of our house at the edge of Chesterfield.

"Good night," Betty said. "Thanks for the movie."

My brother said, "Hurry up. If the folks are awake they might look out and see we're back."

I said "No."

They coaxed, they argued, they scoffed. That is, Betheen and my brother did—for guessable motives wanting me out of the car so they could quickly leave the other two at Betty's door. And when persuasion got them nowhere, they made the mistake of trying to extract me from the rear seat by force.

I was too stubborn to see that nothing remained to be salvaged from my evening. I simply clung and kicked. I grabbed indiscriminately at the upholstery, the window cranks, and Betty. Once I caught big-shouldered Betheen under the chin with my knee. In her recoil she cracked her head on the door frame. A pretty brawl!

They were still tugging uselessly when my father came out. He was wearing his old bathrobe with galoshes over his bare shins. I guess he'd thought we were having some trouble with the car when he started out into the cold.

"Why, you ought to be ashamed," he said to me as he grasped the real nature of our trouble. "Why, Betty's cousin can see that she gets home safe."

"I'd have let him come along if he hadn't put up such a fuss," my brother said. "He kicked Betheen."

"Gee, my mother will worry if I don't get home soon, 'cause tomorrow's a school day," Hudson said.

"Good night," Betty said, with just a precocious hint of sophistication.

Ah, I was ashamed all right. Ashamed of the whole sick, sorry human race as I walked through the frosty yard with my father. The tail lights of the Essex were already disappearing around the corner of the Christian church.

My father threw his arm around my shoulder. He wasn't as foolish or as hypocritical as his remark had made him sound. It was just that he, too, saw no way out of the tangle except to subtract me from it. It had gone beyond considerations of justice. All that remained was to restore order. "You'll see Hudson and Betty at school tomorrow," he said. "You'll see them every day. Thing's 'll go better if you just forget what happened tonight."

I didn't answer.

"Now then, you're too old to cry," he said.

"Well, I'm crying, you bastard."

I expected him to hit me then. In fact you might say I had invited it and would have welcomed the punishment for having been such an idiot.

But he couldn't bring himself to do it. We were standing on the porch by then, and I saw him in fuzzy silhouette against the moonlit yard. I saw him waver as though he were lifting his fist but couldn't quite make it, and then, maybe for the first time, I saw him in his human dimension, bewildered and tugged in contrary directions like me.

"We better get some rest." That was the only moral he could draw from what he had just seen.

You remember that at the end of *Hell's Angels* there is a sequence in a German prison. One of the fly-boy brothers—of course it is the one who *missed* the hanky-panky with Miss Harlow in London that night the zep came over and she got into her comfort suit—has to shoot his sibling with a pilfered Luger to keep him from betraying plans for the spring offensive to the enemy. There's a lot of poetic justice in the shooting. One is made to feel the traitor should have kept it in his pants whatever provocations the Sexual Adversary offered. Morality is vindicated with bookkeeping precision. With the Luger still smoking in his hot little hand, the killer sniffles about *mein bruder* to a baffled Hun.

It has taken me a terrific, lifelong integrative effort to resurrect a memory of that movie with even a tint of morality or poetic justice. The images that first stuck with me composed a very different pattern. That night I lay under the covers sleeplessly waiting for my brother to come home, agonizing the minutes it would take him to get rid of Betty and Hudson, the minutes it would take to wheel down past the elevator for a quick feel and a kiss, and the other minutes to deliver Betheen home and come back.

I had no weapon to commit a physical murder with. But as

plainly as if it were on a silver screen I could see myself hauling a Luger out of the bedclothes as he entered the room and began to undress. I would sneer, *"Mein bruder,"* and let him have it between the eyes. After him, the others, one by one. Then—"spinning through stardust and sunshine"—down I'd go. Down, down, down. Where, after all, my true desires had been tending.

JOY WILLIAMS

TAKING CARE

Third-person narration. *Like the preceding story, this one opens with exposition. It is told in the present tense, a standard but risky device that may enhance a sense of immediacy. The short declarative sentences, however, give a tone of almost clinical detachment—until we note the very highly emotional nature of the subject matter. Perhaps the detachment of the style is a precaution against sentimentality or stock responses to a tale of love, danger and overwhelming tenderness.*

The point of view is mostly confined to what Jones could observe or infer, but there are strange, miniature interjections about his daughter's activities in Mexico that depart from the strict discipline some authors observe in handling point of view.

The episode in which the hare is killed is what Robert Penn Warren calls a symbolic bump—a departure from the story line wherein a compressed miniature of the thematic pattern of the whole is offered. The hare's death is absurd—except for the bewildered wish "to apologize" that it evokes in the man.

The allusion to Mahler's Songs on the Death of Infants *has been placed in the story to generalize the passion that Jones must endure in his privacy.*

The apparently bald style is wrenched, here and there, into metaphors of stunning force. For example: "He is gaunt with belief." Our rational mind rejects this as being literally untrue; our intuitive recognition is that it is radically true.

PB ✗

Jones, the preacher, has been in love all his life. He is baffled by this because as far as he can see, it has never helped anyone, even when they have acknowledged it, which is not often. Jones' love is much too apparent and arouses neglect. He is like an animal in a traveling show who, through some aberration, wears a vital organ outside the skin, awkward and unfortunate, something that shouldn't be seen, certainly something that shouldn't be watched working. Now he sits on a bed beside his wife in the self-care unit of a hospital fifteen miles from their home. She has been committed here for tests. She is so weak, so tired. There is something wrong with her blood. Her arms are covered with bruises where they have gone into the veins. Her hip, too, is blue and swollen where they have drawn out samples of bone marrow. All of this is frightening. The doctors are severe and wise, answering Jones' questions in a way that makes him feel hopelessly deaf. They have told him that there really is no such thing as a disease of the blood, for the blood is not a living tissue but a passive vehicle for the transportation of food, oxygen and waste. They have told him that abnormalities in the blood corpuscles, which his wife seems to have, must be regarded as symptoms of disease elsewhere in the body. They have shown him, upon request, slides and charts of normal and pathological blood cells which look to Jones like canapés. They speak (for he insists) of leukocytosis, myelocytes and megaloblasts. None of this takes into account the love he has for his wife! Jones sits beside her in this dim pleasant room, wearing a gray suit and his clerical collar, for when he leaves her he must visit other parishioners who are patients here. This part of the hospital is like a motel. One may wear one's regular clothes. The rooms have ice–buckets, rugs and colorful bedspreads. How he wishes that they were traveling and staying overnight, this night, in a motel. A nurse comes in with a tiny paper cup full of pills. There are three pills, or rather, capsules, and they are not for his wife but for her blood. The cup is the smallest of its type that Jones has ever seen. All perspective, all sense of time and scale seem abandoned in this hospital. For example, when Jones turns to kiss his wife's hair, he nicks the air instead.

II

Jones and his wife have one child, a daughter, who, in turn, has a single child, a girl, born one-half year ago. Jones' daughter has fallen in with the stars and is using the heavens, as Jones would be the first to admit, more than he ever has. It has, however, brought her only grief and confusion. She has left her husband and brought the baby to Jones. She has also given him her dog, a German shepherd. She is going to Mexico where soon, in the mountains, she will have a nervous breakdown. Jones does not know this, but his daughter has seen it in the stars and is going out to meet it. Jones quickly agrees to care for both the baby and the dog, as this seems to be the only thing his daughter needs from him. The day of the baby's birth is secondary to the position of the planets and the terms of houses, quadrants and gradients. Her symbol is a bareback rider. To Jones, this is a graceful thought. It signifies audacity. It also means luck. Jones slips a twenty dollar bill in the pocket of his daughter's suitcase and drives her to the airport. The plane taxis down the runway and Jones waves, holding all their luck in his arms.

III

One afternoon, Jones had come home and found his wife sitting in the garden, weeping. She had been transplanting flowers, putting them in pots before the first frost came. There was dirt on her forehead and around her mouth. Her light clothes felt so heavy. Their weight made her body ache. Each breath was a stone she had to swallow. She cried and cried in the weak autumn sunshine. Jones could see the veins throbbing in her neck. "I'm dying," she said. "It's taking me months to die." But after he had brought her inside, she insisted that she felt better and made them both a cup of tea while Jones potted the rest of the plants and carried them down cellar. She lay on the sofa and Jones sat beside her. They talked quietly with one another. Indeed, they were almost whispering, as though they were in a public place surrounded by strangers instead of in their own house with no one present but themselves. "It's the season," Jones said. "In fall everything slows down, retreats. I'm feeling tired myself. We need iron. I'll go to the druggist right now and buy some iron tablets." His wife agreed. She wanted to go with him, for the ride. Together they ride, through the towns, for miles and miles, even into the next state. She does not want to stop driving. They buy sandwiches and milkshakes and eat in the car. Jones drives. They have to buy more gasoline. His wife sits close to him, her eyes closed, her head tipped back against the seat. He can see the veins beating on in her neck. Somewhere there is a dreadful sound, almost audible. "First I thought it was my imagination," his wife said. "I couldn't sleep. All night I would stay awake, dreaming. But it's not in my head. It's in my ears, my eyes. They ache. Everything. My tongue. My hair. The tips of my fingers are dead." Jones pressed her cold hand to his lips. He thinks of something mad and loving better than he—running out of control, deeply in the darkness of his wife. "Just don't make me go to the hospital," she pleaded. Of course she will go there. The moment has already occurred.

IV

Jones is writing to his daughter. He received a brief letter from her this morning, telling him where she could be reached. The foreign postmark was so large that it almost obliterated Jones' address. She did not mention either her mother or the baby, which makes Jones feel peculiar. His life seems increated as his God's life, perhaps even imaginary. His daughter tells him about the town in which she lives. She does not plan to stay there long. She wants to travel. She will find out exactly what she wants to do and then she will come home again. The town is poor but interesting and there are many Americans there her own age. There is a zoo right on the beach. Almost all the towns, no matter how small, have little zoos. There are primarily eagles and hawks in the cages. And what can Jones reply to that? He writes *Everything is fine here. We are burning wood from the old apple tree in the fire place and it smells wonderful. Has the baby had her full series of polio shots? Take care.* Jones uses this expression constantly, usually in totally unwarranted situations, as when he purchases pipe cleaners or drives through toll booths. Distracted, Jones writes off the edge of the paper and onto the blotter. He must begin again. He will mail this on the way to the hospital. They have been taking X-rays for three days now but the pictures are cloudy. They cannot read them. His wife is now in a real sickbed with high metal sides. He sits with her while she eats her dinner. She asks him to take her good nightgown home and wash it with a bar of ivory. They won't let her do anything now, not even wash out a few things. *You must take care.*

V

Jones is driving down a country road. It is the first snowfall of the season and he wants to show it to the baby who rides beside him in a small foam-and-metal car seat all her own. Her head is almost on a level with his and she looks earnestly at the landscape, sometimes smiling. They follow the road that winds tightly between fields and deep pine woods. Everything is white and clean. It has been snowing all afternoon and is doing so still, but very very lightly. Fat snowflakes fall solitary against the windshield. Sometimes the baby reaches out for them. Sometimes she gives a brief kick and cry of joy. They have done their errands. Jones has bought milk and groceries and two yellow roses which lie wrapped in tissue and newspaper in the trunk, in the cold. He must buy two on Saturday as the florist is closed on Sunday. He does not like to do this but there is no alternative. The roses do not keep well. Tonight he will give one to his wife. The other he will pack in sugar water and store in the refrigerator. He can only hope that the bud will remain tight until Sunday when he brings it into the terrible heat of the hospital. The baby rocks against the straps of her small carrier. Her lips are pursed as she watches intently the fields, the gray stalks of crops growing out of the snow, the trees. She is warmly dressed and she wears a knitted orange cap. It is twenty-three years old, the age of her mother. Jones found it just the other day when he was looking for it. It has faded almost to pink on one side. At one time, it must have been stored in the sun. Jones, driving, feels almost gay. The snow is so beautiful. Everything is white, even the hood of the car. Jones is an educated man. He has read Melville, who says that white is the colorless all-color of atheism from which we shrink. Jones does not believe this. He sees a holiness in snow, a promise. He hopes that his wife will know that it is snowing even though she is separated from the window by a curtain. Jones sees something moving across the snow, a part of the snow itself, running. Although he is going slowly, he takes his foot completely off the accelerator. "Look, darling, a snowshoe rabbit." At the sound of his voice, the baby stretches open her mouth and narrows her eyes in soundless glee. The hare is splendid. So fast! It flows around invisible obstructions, something out of a kind dream. It flies across the ditch, its paws like paddles, faintly yellow, the color of raw wood. "Look, sweet," cries Jones, "how big he is!" But suddenly the hare is curved and falling, round as a ball, its feet and head tucked closely against its body. It strikes the road and skids upside down for several yards. The car passes around it, avoids it. Jones brakes and stops, amazed. He opens the door and trots back to the animal. The baby twists about in her seat as well as she can and peers after him. It is as though the animal had never been alive at all. Its head is broken in several places. Jones bends to touch its fur, but straightens again, not doing so. A man emerges from the woods, swinging a shotgun. He nods at Jones and picks the hare up by the ears. As he walks away, the hare's legs rub across the ground. There are small crystal stains on the snow. Jones returns to the car. He wants to apologize but he does not know to whom or for what. His life has been devoted to apologetics. It is his profession. He is concerned with both justification and remorse. He has always acted rightly, but nothing has ever come of it. He gets in the car, starts the engine. "Oh, sweet," he says to the baby. She smiles at him, exposing her tooth. At home that night, after the baby's supper, Jones reads a story to her. She is asleep, panting in her sleep, but Jones tells her the story of al–Boraq, the milkwhite steed of Mohammed, who could stride out of the sight of mankind with a single step.

VI

Jones sorts through a collection of records, none of which have been opened. They are still wrapped in cellophane. The jacket designs are subdued, epic. Names, instruments and orchestras are mentioned confidently. He would like to agree with their importance, for he knows that they have worth, but he is not familiar with the references. His daughter brought these records with her. They had been given to her by an older man, a professor she had been having an affair with. Naturally, this pains Jones. His daughter speaks about the men she has been involved with but no longer cares about. Where did these men come from? Where were they waiting and why have they gone? Jones remembers his daughter when she was a little girl, helping him rake leaves. What can he say? For years on April Fool's Day, she would take tobacco out of his humidor and fill it with Corn Flakes. Jones is full of remorse and astonishment. When he saw his daughter only a few weeks ago, she was thin and nervous. She had torn out almost all her eyebrows with her fingers from this nervousness. And her lashes. The roots of her eyes were white, like the bulbs of flowers. Her fingernails were crudely bitten, some bleeding below the quick. She was tough and remote, wanting only to go on a trip for which she had a ticket. What can he do? He seeks her in the face of the baby but she is not there. All is being both continued and resumed, but the dream is different. The dream cannot be revived. Jones breaks into one of the albums, blows the dust from the needle, plays a record. Outside it is dark. The parsonage is remote and the only buildings nearby are barns. The river cannot be seen. The music is Bruckner's *Te Deum*. Very nice. Dedicated to God. He plays the other side. A woman, Kathleen Ferrier, is singing in German. Jones cannot understand the words but the music stuns him. *Kindertotenlieder*. It is devastating. In college he had studied only scientific German, the vocabulary of submarines, dirigibles and steam engines. Jones plays the record again and again, searching for his old grammar. At last he finds it. The wings of insects are between some of the pages. There are notes in pencil, written in his own young hand.

RENDER:

    A. WAS THE TEACHER SATISFIED WITH YOU TODAY?

    B. NO, HE WAS NOT. MY ESSAY WAS GOOD BUT IT WAS NOT COPIED WELL.

    C. I AM SORRY YOU WERE NOT INDUSTRIOUS THIS TIME FOR YOU GENERALLY ARE.

These lessons are neither of life or death. Why was he instructed in them? In the hospital, his wife waits to be translated, no longer a woman, the woman whom he loves, but a situation. Her blood moves mysteriously as constellations. She is under scrutiny and attack and she has abandoned Jones. She is a swimmer waiting to get on with the drowning. Jones is on the shore. In Mexico, his daughter walks along the beach with two men. She is acting out a play that has become her life. Jones is on the mountaintop. The baby cries and Jones takes her from the crib to change her. The dog paws the door. Jones lets him out. He settles down with the baby and listens to the record. *Songs on the Deaths of Infants.* Controlled heartbreak. He still cannot make out many of the words. The baby wiggles restlessly on his lap. Her eyes are a foal's eyes, navy-blue. She has grown in a few weeks to expect everything from Jones. He props her on one edge of the couch and goes to her small toy box where he keeps a bear, a few rattles and balls. On the way, he opens the door and the dog immediately enters. His heavy coat is cold, fragrant with ice. He noses the baby and she squeals.

> *Oft denk' ich, sie sind nur ausgegangen*
> *Bald werden sie wieder nach Hause gelangen*

Jones selects a bright ball and pushes it gently in her direction.

VII

It is Sunday morning and Jones is in the pulpit. The church is very old but the walls of the sanctuary have recently been painted a pale blue. In the cemetery adjoining, some of the graves are three hundred years old. It has become a historical landmark and no one has been buried there since World War I. There is a new place, not far away, which the families now use. Plots are marked not with stones but with small tablets, and immediately after any burial, workmen roll grassed sod over the new graves so that there is no blemish on the grounds, not even for a little while. Present for today's service are seventy-eight adults, eleven children and the junior choir. Jones counts them as the offertory is received. The church rolls say that there are 350 members but as far as Jones can see, everyone is here today. This is the day he baptizes the baby. He has made arrangements with one of the ladies to hold her and bring her up to the font at the end of the first hymn. The baby looks charming in a lacy white dress. Jones has combed her fine hair carefully, slicking it in a curl with water, but now it has dried and it sticks up awkwardly like the crest of a kingfisher. Jones bought the dress in Mammoth Mart, an enormous store which has a large metal elephant dressed in overalls dancing on the roof. He feels foolish at buying it there but he had gone to several stores and that is where he saw the prettiest dress. He blesses the baby with water from the silver bowl. He says, *We are saved not because we are worthy. We are saved because we are loved.* It is a brief ceremony. The baby, looking curiously at Jones, is taken out to the nursery. Jones begins his sermon. He can't remember when he wrote it, but here it is, typed, in front of him. *There is nothing wrong in what one does but there is something wrong in what one becomes.* He finds this questionable but goes on speaking. He has been preaching for thirty-four years. He is gaunt with belief. But his wife has a red cell count of only 2.3 millions. It is not enough! She is not getting enough oxygen! Jones is giving his sermon. Somewhere he has lost what he was looking for. He must have known once, surely. The congregation sways, like the wings of a ray in water. It is Sunday and for patients it is a holiday. The doctors don't visit. There are no tests or diagnoses. Jones would like to leave, to walk down the aisle and out into the winter, where he would read his words into the ground. Why can't he remember his life! He finishes, sits down, stands up to present communion. Tiny cubes of bread lie in a slumped pyramid. They are offered and received. Jones takes his morsel, hacked earlier from a sliced enriched loaf with his own hand. It is so dry, almost wicked.

The very thought now sickens him. He chews it over and over again, but it lies unconsumed, like a muscle in his mouth.

VIII

Jones is waiting in the lobby for the results of his wife's operation. Has there ever been a time before dread? He would be grateful even to have dread back, but it has been lost, for a long time, in rapid possibility, probability and fact. The baby sits on his knees and plays with his tie. She woke very early this morning for her orange juice and then gravely, immediately, spit it all up. She seems fine now, however, her fingers exploring Jones' tie. Whenever he looks at her, she gives him a dazzling smile. He has spent most of the day fiercely cleaning the house, changing the bedsheets and the pages of the many calendars that hang in the rooms, things he should have done a week ago. He has dusted and vacuumed and pressed all his shirts. He has laundered all the baby's clothes, soft small sacks and gowns and sleepers which froze in his hands the moment he stepped outside. And now he is waiting and watching his wristwatch. The tumor is precisely this size, they tell him, the size of his clock's face.

IX

Jones has the baby on his lap and he is feeding her. The evening meal is lengthy and complex. First he must give her vitamins, then, because she has a cold, a dropper of liquid aspirin. This is followed by a bottle of milk, eight ounces, and a portion of strained vegetables. He gives her a rest now so that the food can settle. On his hip, she rides through the rooms of the huge house as Jones turns lights off and on. He comes back to the table and gives her a little more milk, a half jar of strained chicken and a few spoonfuls of dessert, usually cobbler, buckle or pudding. The baby enjoys all equally. She is good. She eats rapidly and neatly. Sometimes she grasps the spoon, turns it around and thrusts the wrong end into her mouth. Of course there is nothing that cannot be done incorrectly.

Jones adores the baby. He sniffs her warm head. Her birth is a deep error, an abstraction. Born in wedlock but out of love. He puts her in the playpen and tends to the dog. He fills one dish with water and one with horsemeat. He rinses out the empty can before putting it in the wastebasket. The dog eats with great civility. He eats a little meat and then takes some water, then meat, then water. When the dog has finished, the dishes are as clean as though they'd been washed. Jones now thinks about his own dinner. He opens the refrigerator. The ladies of the church have brought brownies, venison, cheese and apple sauce. There are turkey pies, pork chops, steak, haddock and sausage patties. A brilliant light exposes all this food. There is so much of it. It must be used. A crust has formed around the punctures in a can of Pet. There is a clear bag of chicken livers stapled shut. There are large brown eggs in a bowl. Jones stares unhappily at the beads of moisture on cartons and bottles, at the pearls of fat on the cold cooked stew. He sits down. The room is full of lamps and cords. He thinks of his wife, her breathing body deranged in tubes, and begins to shake. All objects here are perplexed by such grief.

X

Now it is almost Christmas and Jones is walking down by the river, around an abandoned house. The dog wades heavily through the snow, biting it. There are petals of ice on the tree limbs and when Jones lingers under them, the baby puts out her hand and her mouth starts working because she would like to have it, the ice, the branch, everything. His wife will be coming home in a few days, in time for Christmas. Jones has already put up the tree and brought the ornaments down from the attic. He will not trim it until she comes home. He wants very much to make a fine occasion out of opening the boxes of old decorations. The two of them have always enjoyed this greatly in the past. Jones will doubtlessly drop and smash a bauble, for he does every year. He tramps through the snow with his small voyager. She dangles in a shoulder sling, her legs wedged around his hip. They regard the rotting house seriously.

Once it was a doctor's home and offices but long before Jones' time, the doctor, who was very respected, had been driven away because a town girl accused him of fathering her child. The story goes that all the doctor said was, "Is that so?" This incensed the town and the girl's parents, who insisted that he take the child as soon as it was born. He did and he cared for it very well even though his practice was ruined and no one had anything to do with him. A year later the girl told the truth—that the actual father was a young college boy who she was now going to marry. They wanted the child back, and the doctor willingly gave the infant to them, saying to their apology and confession only, "Is that so?" Of course it is a very old, important story. Jones has always appreciated it, but now he is annoyed at the man's passivity. His wife's sickness has changed everything for Jones. He will continue to accept but he will no longer surrender. Surely things are different for Jones now.

XI

For insurance purposes, Jones' wife is brought out to the car in a wheelchair. She is thin and beautiful. Jones is grateful and confused. He has a mad wish to tip the orderly. Have so many years really passed? Is this not his wife, his love, fresh from giving birth? Isn't everything about to begin? In Mexico, his daughter wanders disinterestedly through a jewelry shop where she picks up a small silver egg. It opens on a hinge and inside are two figures, a bride and groom. Jones puts the baby in his wife's arms. At first the baby is alarmed because she cannot remember this person very well and she reaches for Jones, whimpering. But soon she is soothed by his wife's soft voice and she falls asleep in her arms as they drive. Jones has readied everything carefully for his wife's homecoming. The house is clean and orderly. For days he has restricted himself to only one part of the house so that his clutter will be minimal. Jones helps his wife up the steps to the door. Together they enter the shining rooms.

ANTON CHEKHOV

THE LADY WITH THE PET DOG

19 century language.

Third-person narration. *The story is realistic, but the presentation is not particularly* objective. *Here we find the* omniscient author *expounding the details and the generalities of Gurov's thought, character, and milieu. The story is told from Gurov's* point of view, *but the author does not limit himself to Gurov's thought or experiences.*

The plot *is submerged. It may seem to you that there is no plot, but if you pay attention to the phases through which Gurov passes you will see its firm structure under the fluid surface.*

The settings *are used to hint the changes of mood and circumstance through which Gurov passes.*

The ironic, melancholy tone *rises chiefly, perhaps, from the surprises of the plot, but is enhanced by some of the rueful observations contributed by the author.*

Note that this is the only story in this book which was not originally written in English, and the only one written before 1960. Be on guard against picking up usages from this story that may be accidents of translation or somewhat outmoded fashions of narration.

A new person, it was said, had appeared on the esplanade: a lady with a pet dog. Dmitry Dmitrich Gurov, who had spent a fortnight at Yalta and had got used to the place, had also begun to take an interest in new arrivals. As he sat in Vernet's confectionery shop, he saw, walking on the esplanade, a fair-haired young woman of medium height, wearing a beret; a white Pomeranian was trotting behind her.

And afterwards he met her in the public garden and in the square several times a day. She walked alone, always wearing the same beret and always with the white dog; no one knew who she was and everyone called her simply "the lady with the pet dog."

"If she is here alone without husband or friends," Gurov reflected, "it wouldn't be a bad thing to make her acquaintance."

He was under forty, but he already had a daughter twelve years old, and two sons at school. They had found a wife for him when he was very young, a student in his second year, and by now she seemed half as old again as he. She was a tall, erect woman with dark eyebrows, stately and dignified and, as she said of herself, intellectual. She read a great deal, used simplified spelling in her letters, called her husband, not Dmitry, but Dimitry, while he privately considered her of limited intelligence, narrow-minded, dowdy, was afraid of her, and did not like to be at home. He had begun being unfaithful to her long ago—had been unfaithful to her often and, probably for that reason, almost always spoke ill of women, and when they were talked of in his presence used to call them "the inferior race."

It seemed to him that he had been sufficiently tutored by bitter experience to call them what he pleased, and yet he could not have lived without "the inferior race" for two days together. In the company of men he was bored and ill at ease, he was chilly and uncommunicative with them; but when he was among women he felt free, and knew what to speak to them about and how to comport himself; and even to be silent with them was no strain on him. In his appearance, in his character, in his whole make-up there was something attractive and elusive that disposed women in his favor and allured them. He knew that, and some force seemed to draw him to them, too.

Oft-repeated and really bitter experience had taught him long ago that with decent people—particularly Moscow people—who are irresolute and slow to move, every affair which at first seems a light and charming adventure inevitably grows into a whole problem of extreme complexity, and in the end a painful situation is created. But at every new meeting with an interesting woman this lesson of experience seemed to slip from his memory, and he was eager for life, and everything seemed so simple and diverting.

One evening while he was dining in the public garden the lady in the beret walked up without haste to take the next table. Her expression, her gait, her dress, and the way she did her hair told him that she belonged to the upper class, that she was married, that she was in Yalta for the first time and alone, and that she was bored there. The stories told of the immorality in Yalta are to a great extent untrue; he despised them, and knew that such stories were made up for the most part by persons who would have been glad to sin themselves if they had had the chance; but when the lady sat down at the next table three paces from him, he recalled these stories of easy conquests, of trips to the mountains, and the tempting thought of a swift, fleeting liaison, a romance with an unknown woman of whose very name he was ignorant suddenly took hold of him.

He beckoned invitingly to the Pomeranian, and when the dog approached him, shook his finger at it. The Pomeranian growled; Gurov threatened it again.

The lady glanced at him and at once dropped her eyes.

"He doesn't bite," she said and blushed.

"May I give him a bone?" he asked; and when she nodded he inquired affably, "Have you been in Yalta long?"

"About five days."

"And I am dragging out the second week here."

There was a short silence.

"Time passes quickly, and yet it is so dull here!" she said, not looking at him.

"It's only the fashion to say it's dull here. A provincial will live in Belyov or Zhizdra and not be bored, but when he comes here it's 'Oh, the dullness! Oh, the dust!' One would think he came from Granada."

She laughed. Then both continued eating in silence, like strangers, but after dinner they walked together and there sprang up between them the light banter of people who are free and contented, to whom it does not matter where they go or what they talk about. They walked and talked of the strange light on the sea: the water was a soft, warm, lilac color, and there was a golden band of moonlight upon it. They talked of how sultry it was after a hot day. Gurov told her that he was a native of Moscow, that he had studied languages and literature at the university, but had a post in a bank; that at one time he had trained to become an opera singer but had given it up, that he owned two houses in Moscow. And he learned from her that she had grown up in Petersburg, but had lived in S— since her marriage two years previously, that she was going to stay in Yalta for about another month, and that her husband, who needed a rest, too, might perhaps come to fetch her. She was not certain whether her husband was a member of a Government Board or served on a Zemstvo Council, and this amused her. And Gurov learned too that her name was Anna Sergeyevna.

Afterwards in his room at the hotel he thought about her—and was certain that he would meet her the next day. It was bound to happen. Getting into bed he recalled that she had been a schoolgirl only recently, doing lessons like his own daughter; he thought how much timidity and angularity there was still in her laugh and her manner of talking with a stranger. It must have been the first time in her life that she was alone in a setting in which she was followed, looked at, and spoken to for one secret purpose alone, which she could hardly fail to guess. He thought of her slim, delicate throat, her lovely gray eyes.

"There's something pathetic about her, though," he thought, and dropped off.

II

A week had passed since they had struck up an acquaintance. It was a holiday. It was close indoors, while in the street the wind whirled the dust about and blew people's hats off. One was thirsty all day, and Gurov often went into the restaurant and offered Anna Sergeyevna a soft drink or ice cream. One did not know what to do with oneself.

In the evening when the wind had abated they went out on the pier to watch the steamer come in. There were a great many people walking about the dock; they had come to welcome someone and they were carrying bunches of flowers. And two peculiarities of a festive Yalta crowd stood out: the elderly ladies were dressed like young ones and there were many generals.

Owing to the choppy sea, the steamer arrived late, after sunset, and it was a long time tacking about before it put in at the pier. Anna Sergeyevna peered at the steamer and the passengers through her lorgnette as though looking for acquaintances, and whenever she turned to Gurov her eyes were shining. She talked a great deal and asked questions jerkily, forgetting the next moment what she had asked; then she lost her lorgnette in the crush.

The festive crowd began to disperse; it was now too dark to see people's faces; there was no wind any more, but Gurov and Anna Sergeyevna still stood as though waiting to see someone else come off the steamer. Anna Sergeyevna was silent now, and sniffed her flowers without looking at Gurov.

"The weather has improved this evening," he said. "Where shall we go now? Shall we drive somewhere?"

She did not reply.

Then he looked at her intently, and suddenly embraced her and kissed her on the lips, and the moist fragrance of her flowers enveloped him; and at once he looked round him anxiously, wondering if anyone had seen them.

"Let us go to your place," he said softly. And they walked off together rapidly.

The air in her room was close and there was the smell of the perfume she had bought at the Japanese shop. Looking at her, Gurov thought: "What encounters life offers!" From the past he preserved the memory of carefree, good-natured women whom love made gay and who were grateful to him for the happiness he gave them, however brief it might be; and of women like his wife who loved without sincerity, with too many words, affectedly, hysterically, with an expression that it was not love or passion that engaged them but something more significant; and of two or three others, very beautiful, frigid women, across whose faces would suddenly flit a rapacious expression—an obstinate desire to take from life more than it could give, and these were women no longer young, capricious, unreflecting, domineering, unintelligent, and when Gurov grew cold to them their beauty aroused his hatred, and the lace on their lingerie seemed to him to resemble scales.

But here there was the timidity, the angularity of inexperienced youth, a feeling of awkwardness; and there was a sense of embarrassment, as though someone had suddenly knocked at the door. Anna Sergeyevna, "the lady with the pet dog," treated what had happened in a peculiar way, very seriously, as though it were her fall—so it seemed, and this was odd and inappropriate. Her features drooped and faded, and her long hair hung down sadly on either side of her face; she grew pensive and her dejected pose was that of a Magdalene in a picture by an old master.

"It's not right," she said. "You don't respect me now, you first of all."

There was a watermelon on the table. Gurov cut himself a slice and began eating it without haste. They were silent for at least half an hour.

There was something touching about Anna Sergeyevna; she had the purity of a well-bred, naive woman who has seen little of life. The single candle burning on the table barely illumined her face, yet it was clear that she was unhappy.

"Why should I stop respecting you, darling?" asked Gurov. "You don't know what you're saying."

"God forgive me," she said, and her eyes filled with tears. "It's terrible."

"It's as though you were trying to exonerate yourself."

"How can I exonerate myself? No. I am a bad, low woman; I despise myself and I have no thought of exonerating myself. It's not my husband but myself I have deceived. And not only just now; I have been deceiving myself for a long time. My husband may be a good, honest man, but he is a flunkey! I don't know what he does, what his work is, but I know he is a flunkey! I was twenty when I married him. I was tormented by curiosity; I wanted something better. 'There must be a different sort of life,' I said to myself. I wanted to live! To live, to live! Curiosity kept eating at me—you don't understand it, but I swear to God I could no longer control myself; something was going on in me; I could not be held back. I told my husband I was ill, and came here. And here I have been walking about as though in a daze, as though I were mad; and now I have become a vulgar, vile woman whom anyone may despise."

Gurov was already bored with her; he was irritated by her naive tone, by her repentance, so unexpected and so out of place, but for the tears in her eyes he might have thought she was joking or play-acting.

"I don't understand, my dear," he said softly. "What do you want?"

She hid her face on his breast and pressed close to him.

"Believe me, believe me, I beg you," she said, "I love honesty and purity, and sin is loathsome to me; I don't know what I'm doing. Simple people say, 'The Evil One has led me astray.' And I may say of myself now that the Evil One has led me astray."

"Quiet, quiet," he murmured.

He looked into her fixed, frightened eyes, kissed her, spoke to her softly and affectionately, and by degrees she calmed down, and her gaiety returned; both began laughing.

Afterwards when they went out there was not a soul on the esplanade. The town with its cypresses looked quite dead, but the sea was still sounding as it broke upon the beach; a single launch was rocking on the waves and on it a lantern was blinking sleepily.

They found a cab and drove to Oreanda.

"I found out your surname in the hall just now: it was written on the board—von Dideritz," said Gurov. "Is your husband German?"

"No; I believe his grandfather was German, but he is Greek Orthodox himself."

At Oreanda they sat on a bench not far from the church, looked down at the sea, and were silent. Yalta was barely visible through the morning mist; white clouds rested motionlessly on the mountaintops. The leaves did not stir on the trees, cicadas twanged, and the monotonous muffled sound of the sea that rose from below spoke of the peace, the eternal sleep awaiting us. So it rumbled below when there was no Yalta, no Oreanda here; so it rumbles now, and it will rumble as indifferently and as hollowly when we are no more.

And in this constancy, in this complete indifference to the life and death of each of us, there lies, perhaps, a pledge of our eternal salvation, of the unceasing advance of life upon earth, of unceasing movement towards perfection. Sitting beside a young woman who in the dawn seemed so lovely, Gurov, soothed and spellbound by these magical surroundings—the sea, the mountains, the clouds, the wide sky—thought how everything is really beautiful in this world when one reflects: everything except what we think or do ourselves when we forget the higher aims of life and our own human dignity.

A man strolled up to them—probably a guard—looked at them and walked away. And this detail, too, seemed so mysterious and beautiful. They saw a steamer arrive from Feodosia, its lights extinguished in the glow of dawn.

"There is dew on the grass," said Anna Sergeyevna, after a silence.

"Yes, it's time to go home."

They returned to the city.

Then they met every day at twelve o'clock on the esplanade, lunched and dined together, took walks, admired the sea. She complained that she slept badly, that she had palpitations, asked the same questions, troubled now by jealousy and now by the fear that he did not respect her sufficiently. And often in the square or the public garden, when there was no one near them, he suddenly drew her to him and kissed her passionately. Complete idleness, these kisses in broad daylight exchanged furtively in dread of someone's seeing them, the heat, the smell of the sea, and the continual flitting before his eyes of idle, well-dressed, well-fed people, worked a complete change in him; he kept telling Anna Sergeyevna how beautiful she was, how seductive, was urgently passionate; he would not move a step away from her, while she was often pensive and continually pressed him to confess that he did not respect her, did not love her in the least, and saw in her nothing but a common woman. Almost every evening rather late they drove somewhere out of town, to Oreanda or to the waterfall; and the excursion was always a success, the scenery invariably impressed them as beautiful and magnificent.

They were expecting her husband, but a letter came from him saying that he had eye-trouble, and begging his wife to return home as soon as possible. Anna Sergeyevna made haste to go.

"It's a good thing I am leaving," she said to Gurov. "It's the hand of Fate!"

She took a carriage to the railway station, and he went with her. They were driving the whole day. When she had taken her place in the express, and when the second bell had rung, she said, "Let me look at you once more—let me look at you again. Like this."

She was not crying but was so sad that she seemed ill and her face was quivering.

"I shall be thinking of you—remembering you," she said. "God bless you; be happy. Don't remember evil against me. We are parting forever—it has to be, for we ought never to have met. Well, God bless you."

The train moved off rapidly, its lights soon vanished, and a minute later there was no sound of it, as though everything had conspired to end as quickly as possible that sweet trance, that madness. Left alone on the platform, and gazing into the dark distance, Gurov listened to the twang of the grasshoppers and the hum of the telegraph wires, feeling as though he had just waked up. And he reflected, musing, that there had now been another episode or adventure in his life, and it, too, was at an end, and nothing was left of it but a memory. He was moved, sad, and slightly remorseful: this young woman whom he would never meet again had not been happy with him; he had been warm and affectionate with her, but yet in his manner, his tone, and his caresses there had been a shade of light irony, the slightly coarse arrogance of a happy male who was, besides, almost twice her age. She had constantly called him kind, exceptional, high-minded; obviously he had seemed to her different from what he really was, so he had involuntarily deceived her.

Here at the station there was already a scent of autumn in the air; it was a chilly evening.

"It is time for me to go north, too," thought Gurov as he left the platform. "High time!"

III

At home in Moscow the winter routine was already established; the stoves were heated, and in the morning it was still dark when the children were having breakfast and getting ready for school, and the nurse would light the lamp for a short time. There were frosts already. When the first snow falls, on the first day the sleighs are out, it is pleasant to see the white earth, the white roofs; one draws easy, delicious breaths, and the season brings back the days of one's youth. The old limes and birches, white with hoar-frost, have a good-natured look; they are closer to one's heart than cypresses and palms, and near them one no longer wants to think of mountains and the sea.

Gurov, a native of Moscow, arrived there on a fine frosty day, and when he put on his fur coat and warm gloves and took a walk along Petrovka, and when on Saturday night he heard the bells ringing, his recent trip and the places he had visited lost all charm for him. Little by little he became immersed in Moscow life, greedily read three newspapers a day, and declared that he did not read the Moscow papers on principle. He already felt a longing for restaurants, clubs, formal dinners, anniversary celebrations, and it flattered him to entertain distinguished lawyers and actors, and to play cards with a professor at the physicians' club. He could eat a whole portion of meat stewed with pickled cabbage and served in a pan, Moscow style.

A month or so would pass and the image of Anna Sergeyevna, it seemed to him, would become misty in his memory, and only from time to time he would dream of her with her touching smile as he dreamed of others. But more than a month went by, winter came into its own, and everything was still clear in his memory as though he had parted from Anna Sergeyevna only yesterday. And his memories glowed more and more vividly. When in the evening stillness the voices of his children preparing their lessons reached his study, or when he listened to a song or to an organ playing in a restaurant, or when the storm howled in the chimney, suddenly everything would rise up in his memory; what had happened on the pier and the early morning with the mist on the mountains, and the steamer coming from Feodosia, and the kisses. He would pace about his room a long time, remembering and smiling; then his memories passed into reveries, and in his imagination the past would mingle with what was to come. He did not dream of Anna Sergeyevna, but she followed him about everywhere and watched him. When he shut his eyes he saw her before him as though she were there in the flesh, and she seemed to him lovelier, younger, tenderer than she had been, and he imagined himself a finer man than he had been in Yalta. Of evenings she peered out at him from the bookcase, from the fireplace, from the corner—he heard her breathing, the caressing rustle of her clothes. In the street he followed the women with his eyes, looking for someone who resembled her.

Already he was tormented by a strong desire to share his memories with someone. But in his home it was impossible to talk of his love, and he had no one to talk to outside; certainly he could not confide in his tenants or in anyone at the bank. And what was there to talk about? He hadn't loved her then, had he? Had there been anything beautiful, poetical, edifying, or simply interesting in his relations with Anna Sergeyevna? And he was forced to talk vaguely of love, of women, and no one guessed what he meant; only his wife would twitch her black eyebrows and say, "The part of a philanderer does not suit you at all, Dimitry."

One evening, coming out of the physicians' club with an official with whom he had been playing cards, he could not resist saying:

"If you only knew what a fascinating woman I became acquainted with at Yalta!"

The official got into his sledge and was driving away, but turned suddenly and shouted:

"Dmitry Dmitrich!"

"What is it?"   *very interesting dialogue*

"You were right this evening: the sturgeon was a bit high." →

These words, so commonplace, for some reason moved Gurov to indignation, and struck him as degrading and unclean. What savage manners, what mugs! What stupid nights, what dull, humdrum days! Frenzied gambling, gluttony, drunkenness, continual talk always about the same thing! Futile pursuits and conversations always about the same topics take up the better part of one's time, the better part of one's strength, and in the end there is left a life clipped and wingless, an absurd mess, and there is no escaping or getting away from it—just as though one were in a madhouse or a prison.

Gurov, boiling with indignation, did not sleep all night. And he had a headache all the next day. And the following nights too he slept badly; he sat up in bed, thinking, or paced up and down his room. He was fed up with his children, fed up with the bank; he had no desire to go anywhere or to talk of anything.

In December during the holidays he prepared to take a trip and told his wife he was going to Petersburg to do what he could for a young friend—and he set off for S—. What for? He did not know, himself. He wanted to see Anna Sergeyevna and talk with her, to arrange a rendezvous if possible.

He arrived at S— in the morning, and at the hotel took the best room, in which the floor was covered with gray army cloth, and on the table there was an inkstand, gray with dust and topped by a figure on horseback, its hat in its raised hand and its head broken off. The porter gave him the necessary information: von Dideritz lived in a house of his own on Staro-Goncharnaya Street, not far from the hotel: he was rich and lived well and kept his own horses; everyone in the town knew him. The porter pronounced the name: "Dridiritz."

Without haste Gurov made his way to Staro-Goncharnaya Street and found the house. Directly opposite the house stretched a long gray fence studded with nails.

"A fence like that would make one run away," thought Gurov, looking now at the fence, now at the windows of the house.

He reflected: this was a holiday, and the husband was apt to be at home. And in any case, it would be tactless to go into the house and disturb her. If he were to send her a note, it might fall into her husband's hands, and that might spoil everything. The best thing was to rely on chance. And he kept walking up and down the street and along the fence, waiting for the chance. He saw a beggar go in at the gate and heard the dogs attack him; then an hour later he heard a piano, and the sound came to him faintly and indistinctly.

Probably it was Anna Sergeyevna playing. The front door opened suddenly, and an old woman came out, followed by the familiar white Pomeranian. Gurov was on the point of calling to the dog, but his heart began beating violently, and in his excitement he could not remember the Pomeranian's name.

He kept walking up and down, and hated the gray fence more and more, and by now he thought irritably that Anna Sergeyevna had forgotten him, and was perhaps already diverting herself with another man, and that that was very natural in a young woman who from morning till night had to look at that damn fence. He went back to his hotel room and sat on the couch for a long while, not knowing what to do, then he had dinner and a long nap.

"How stupid and annoying all this is!" he thought when he woke and looked at the dark windows: it was already evening. "Here I've had a good sleep for some reason. What am I going to do at night?"

He sat on the bed, which was covered with a cheap gray blanket of the kind seen in hospitals, and he twitted himself in his vexation:

"So there's your lady with the pet dog. There's your adventure. A nice place to cool your heels in."

That morning at the station a playbill in large letters had caught his eye. *The Geisha* was to be given for the first time. He thought of this and drove to the theater.

"It's quite possible that she goes to first nights," he thought.

The theater was full. As in all provincial theaters, there was a haze above the chandelier, the gallery was noisy and restless; in the front row, before the beginning of the performance the local dandies were standing with their hands clasped behind their backs; in the Governor's box the Governor's daughter, wearing a boa, occupied the front seat, while the Governor himself hid modestly behind the portiere and only his hands were visible; the curtain swayed; the orchestra was a long time tuning up. While the audience was coming in and taking their seats, Gurov scanned the faces eagerly.

Anna Sergeyevna, too, came in. She sat down in the third row, and when Gurov looked at her his heart contracted, and he understood clearly that in the whole world there was no human being so near, so precious, and so important to him; she, this little, undistinguished woman, lost in a provincial crowd, with a vulgar lorgnette in her hand, filled his whole life now, was his sorrow and his joy, the only happiness that he now desired for himself, and to the sounds of the bad orchestra, of the miserable local violins, he thought how lovely she was. He thought and dreamed.

A young man with small side-whiskers, very tall and stooped, came in with Anna Sergeyevna and sat down beside her; he nodded his head at every step and seemed to be bowing continually. Probably this was the husband whom at Yalta, in an access of bitter feeling, she had called a flunkey. And there really was in his lanky figure, his side-whiskers, his small bald patch, something of a flunkey's retiring manner; his smile was mawkish, and in his buttonhole there was an academic badge like a waiter's number.

During the first intermission the husband went out to have a smoke; she remained in her seat. Gurov, who was also sitting in the orchestra, went up to her and said in a shaky voice, with a forced smile:

"Good evening!"

She glanced at him and turned pale, then looked at him again in horror, unable to believe her eyes, and gripped the fan and the lorgnette tightly together in her hands, evidently trying to keep herself from fainting. Both were silent. She was sitting, he was standing, frightened by her distress and not daring to take a seat beside her. The violins and the flute that were being tuned up sang out. He suddenly felt frightened: it seemed as if all the people in the boxes were looking at them. She got up and went hurriedly to the exit; he followed her, and both of them walked blindly along the corridors and up and down stairs, and figures in the uniforms prescribed for magistrates, teachers, and officials of the Department of Crown Lands, all wearing badges, flitted before their eyes, as did also ladies, and fur coats on hangers; they were conscious of drafts and the smell of stale tobacco. And Gurov, whose heart was beating violently, thought:

"Oh, Lord! Why are these people here and this orchestra!"

And at that instant he suddenly recalled how when he had seen Anna Sergeyevna off at the station he had said to himself that all was over between them and that they would never meet again. But how distant the end still was!

On the narrow, gloomy staircase over which it said "To the Amphitheatre," she stopped.

"How you frightened me!" she said, breathing hard, still pale and stunned. "Oh, how you frightened me! I am barely alive. Why did you come? Why?"

"But do understand, Anna, do understand—" he said hurriedly, under his breath. "I implore you, do understand—"

She looked at him with fear, with entreaty, with love; she looked at him intently, to keep his features more distinctly in her memory.

"I suffer so," she went on, not listening to him. "All this time I have been thinking of nothing but you; I live only by the thought of you. And I wanted to forget, to forget; but why, oh, why have you come?"

On the landing above them two high school boys were looking down and smoking, but it was all the same to Gurov; he drew Anna Sergeyevna to him and began kissing her face and her hands.

"What are you doing, what are you doing!" she was saying in horror, pushing him away. "We have lost our senses. Go away today; go away at once— I conjure you by all that is sacred, I implore you— People are coming this way!"

Someone was walking up the stairs.

"You must leave," Anna Sergeyevna went on in a whisper. "Do you hear, Dmitry Dmitrich? I will come and see you in Moscow. I have never been happy; I am unhappy now, and I never, never shall be happy, never! So don't make me suffer still more! I swear I'll come to Moscow. But now let us part. My dear, good, precious one, let us part!"

She pressed his hand and walked rapidly downstairs, turning to look round at him, and from her eyes he could see that she really was unhappy. Gurov stood for a while, listening, then when all grew quiet, he found his coat and left the theater.

IV

And Anna Sergeyevna began coming to see him in Moscow. Once every two or three months she left S— telling her husband that she was going to consult a doctor about a woman's ailment from which she was suffering—and her husband did and did not believe her. When she arrived in Moscow she would stop at the Slavyansky Bazar Hotel, and at once send a man in a red cap to Gurov. Gurov came to see her, and no one in Moscow knew of it.

Once he was going to see her in this way on a winter morning (the messenger had come the evening before and not found him in). With him walked his daughter, whom he wanted to take to school; it was on the way. Snow was coming down in big wet flakes.

"It's three degrees above zero, and yet it's snowing," Gurov was saying to his daughter. "But this temperature prevails only on the surface of the earth; in the upper layers of the atmosphere there is quite a different temperature."

"And why doesn't it thunder in winter, papa?"

He explained that, too. He talked, thinking all the while that he was on his way to a rendezvous, and no living soul knew of it, and probably no one would ever know. He had two lives, an open one, seen and known by all who needed to know it, full of conventional truth and conventional falsehood, exactly like the lives of his friends and acquaintances; and another life that went on in secret. And through some strange, perhaps accidental, combination of circumstances, everything that was of interest and importance to him, everything that was essential to him, everything about which he felt sincerely and did not deceive himself, everything that constituted the core of his life, was going on concealed from others; while all that was false, the shell in which he hid to cover the truth—his work at the bank, for instance, his discussions at the club, his references to the "inferior race," his appearances at anniversary celebrations with his wife—all that went on in the open. Judging others by himself, he did not believe what he saw, and always fancied that every man led his real, most interesting life under cover of secrecy as under cover of night. The personal life of every individual is based on secrecy, and perhaps it is partly for that reason that civilized man is so nervously anxious that personal privacy should be respected.

Having taken his daughter to school, Gurov went on to the Slavyansky Bazar Hotel. He took off his fur coat in the lobby, went upstairs, and knocked gently at the door. Anna Sergeyevna, wearing his favorite gray dress, exhausted by the journey and by waiting, had been expecting him since the previous evening. She was pale, and looked at him without a smile, and he had hardly entered when she flung herself on his breast. That kiss was a long, lingering one, as though they had not seen one another for two years.

"Well, darling, how are you getting on there?" he asked. "What news?"

"Wait; I'll tell you in a moment— I can't speak."

She could not speak; she was crying. She turned away from him, and pressed her handkerchief to her eyes.

"Let her have her cry; meanwhile I'll sit down," he thought, and he seated himself in an armchair.

Then he rang and ordered tea, and while he was having his tea she remained standing at the window with her back to him. She was crying out of sheer agitation, in the sorrowful consciousness that their life was so sad; that they could only see each other in secret and had to hide from people like thieves! Was it not a broken life?

"Come, stop now, dear!" he said.

It was plain to him that this love of theirs would not be over soon, that the end of it was not in sight. Anna Sergeyevna was growing more and more attached to him. She adored him, and it was unthinkable to tell her that their love was bound to come to an end some day; besides, she would not have believed it!

He went up to her and took her by the shoulders, to fondle her and say something diverting, and at that moment he caught sight of himself in the mirror.

His hair was already beginning to turn gray. And it seemed odd to him that he had grown so much older in the last few years, and lost his looks. The shoulders on which his hands rested were warm and heaving. He felt compassion for this life, still so warm and lovely, but probably already about to begin to fade and wither like his own. Why did she love him so much? He always seemed to women different from what he was, and they loved in him not himself, but the man whom their imagination created and whom they had been eagerly seeking all their lives; and afterwards, when they saw their mistake, they loved him nevertheless. And not one of them had been happy with him. In the past he had met women, come together with them, parted from them, but he had never once loved; it was anything you please, but not love. And only now when his head was gray he had fallen in love, really, truly—for the first time in his life.

Anna Sergeyevna and he loved each other as people do who are very close and intimate, like man and wife, like tender friends; it seemed to them that Fate itself had meant them for one another, and they could not understand why he had a wife and she a husband; and it was as though they were a pair of migratory birds, male and female, caught and forced to live in different cages. They forgave each other what they were ashamed of in their past, they forgave everything in the present, and felt that this love of theirs had altered them both.

Formerly in moments of sadness he had soothed himself with whatever logical arguments came into his head, but now he no longer cared for logic; he felt profound compassion, he wanted to be sincere and tender.

"Give it up now, my darling," he said. "You've had your cry; that's enough. Let us have a talk now, we'll think up something."

Then they spent a long time taking counsel together, they talked of how to avoid the necessity for secrecy, for deception, for living in different cities, and not seeing one another for long stretches of time. How could they free themselves from these intolerable fetters?

"How? How?" he asked, clutching his head. "How?"

And it seemed as though in a little while the solution would be found, and then a new and glorious life would begin; and it was clear to both of them that the end was still far off, and that what was to be most complicated and difficult for them was only just beginning.

" love is not happy in this story ⊕ especial for G & Anna

JAMES B. HALL

US HE DEVOURS

This story is a fantasy—*but it is a fantasy derived from reality and myth. I have heard the author say that the basic circumstances of the spinster's embezzlement were found in a newspaper story, one of those eccentric bits of fact for which journalism offers no sufficient explanation. No doubt, in reality, the police sought a* motive *for her crime. So did the writer of this story, deliberately breaking beyond the boundaries of the shallow psychology and practical metaphysics that police are supposed to employ in an effort to expose the root of motivation planted in the deep soil of the collective unconsciousness.*

Though the story is told in the third person, clearly the language is adapted *and* heightened *to give a sense of the ecstatic frenzy bubbling under Miss Festner's superficial decorum.*

Note that the author never testifies directly to the existence of the divine goat. It is Miss Festner who hears it cough and nibble branches. Is this hallucination or mystic perception? Part of the humor of the performance is the author's tactic of leaving this question unanswered.

The goat coughed in the tree outside her window.

Oh she had waited so long to see the hoofs firm upon the lowest branches, the flanks slender, stretched upward among the catalpa leaves, the head half concealed, the backward curving horns erect, glistening in the moist light of the moon.

Miss Festner had thought all these times were past, forever, but now her branches rustled louder, and she stiffened in her bed. Stringy and coarse and rancid as a chicken house floor, the odor afloat in the catalpa tree came to her. She lay in her bed and she felt her back and her thighs harden. This time she was determined to wait.

From experience Miss Festner knew that to leap from her bed, to rush to the casement, to cry out, was useless. When younger she had cried out, in fear; later she knew she must wait without emotion. Not always did the goat leap with a terrible cracking of small branches, and scramble pawing across her window sill.

Sometimes it came—perhaps silently—then deserted her. Sometimes the cry of reed pipes swelled inside her room until her ears and heart and her hard breasts ached; sometimes, after the cry of the loon and after the last crackling noise of great weight among branches, it went away. If it awakened her, and then deserted her, she would go to her window and stare out across the town, which fell away below her windows toward the river. Therefore she did not now dare look toward the window when the odor of stalls and rabbit hutches and stables came to her like smoke from the leaves of the shimmering tree.

For this it seemed she had been waiting a very long time. She had almost given up hope, but now she did what she could. Her quick money-counting fingers dug deeper into the little holes in the farthest edges of her mattress. The sheet across her knees and thighs and her dry belly made spasms of motion.

Some things she could not control, but some things she could do: always she left her window open, she used only the lightest of sheets, and always she was *clean, clean.* If she looked now the eyes she might see would flee into the kingdom of her dreams. But oh tonight she could not wait.

With her eyes still closed she threw the small sheet from her body. Exposed. Yes and on display and naked as the first day her quick money-counting fingers worked inside her Teller's cage. From Escrows in the bank, she had gone behind a Teller's window. Since then she had her window at the bank, with bars, and the businessmen of the town came to her with money and she handled each day the hard, hand-fitting, phallic rolls of dimes, nickels, and quarters. That night in spring, for the first time, the goat coughed in the catalpa tree in the yard of her small house and in her inexperience and her fear she had run too quickly to her bedroom window and the musk-scented thing had fled somewhere across the roiled shadows of her yard.

Finally she learned to wait motionless in her bed, for only then would the wool–soft yarn and the perfume and the polished mother–of–pearl horns and the soft resilient body—only then would it stay lovely as flowers unfolding beside and over her until the dawn humming awoke in her arms. Those mornings she telephoned Mr. Nelscot at the bank. She did not go down the hill to sit behind the window of her Teller's cage until after her lunch.

Louder now outside her bedroom window the small branches shattered. Was now the time, this night?

In the catalpa tree outside she heard it whet the saber of its horns against the topmost branches. Were the hoarse violent eyes staring at her now?

She resisted a moment, and then she no longer cared. To see, to glimpse it among branches seemed enough. She opened wide her eyes.

No. Not there. Gone.

The cry of the loon in the frozen trees chilled her. She had been terribly hot; now she was not hot. She felt more deserted, and more forlorn, than ever before. Yet she was not and never could be sinfully passive, for urgency even in her waking hours grew like a fuse somewhere inside her. She recognized, she even welcomed, the desperation that came galloping to her. She knew she must go out, must seek, must search once more.

Of late when the goat coughed in the branches outside her window and then deserted her, she had followed. Once she had been astonished at her own headlong urgency, but she had gone on because she believed that in frenzy was the hot little kernel of satisfaction. Now that restraint was somewhere far behind her she could think of nothing at all except a highway, twisting somewhere ahead.

II

Furiously she drove the country, limestone roads. Ahead on a curve the guardrails writhed in her headlight beams. At a crossroad she saw the shadow of a country mailbox lie black beside some farmer's lane, and as she passed the black check mark shadow seemed to fade, and then to become a check mark of flame in the corner of her headlong eye.

The constant search, it was, that vexed her. At one time the first place she stopped was always the right place. But as the years fled her, she found the right place was now always farther away, until now she was resigned to the longest drive of all: this night she knew without caring that she would go far beyond a familiar tilt-roofed, ramshackle barn that roosted in a pasture, reviled even by the shoat's moist farming nose.

One spring she had first gone outside. She had gone directly to a certain creek that divided two meadows, where a sand bar of supine luminous tissues of gravel lay exposed between rocks and the water. Later she found her sand bar was not the right place and she had to drive on to a field freshly harrowed, and then on still farther, in the fall, to a place of stubbles, of wheat lately under the sickle bars of harvest. From habit, or from some terrible wish, she still drove first to the sand bar and then to the fields, in the order of their discovery. Finally she came to a familiar bridge. Across this bridge was a grove of oaks that was lovely and dark and deep, a mat of green between two hills.

The planks of the bridge seemed to say this was the place that she must find. But she could accept no comfort from the mutter of planks. Always, until the final moment, there was uncertainty. Suppose the place now had to be still more remote, a place where she could never travel, a place so cleverly concealed in a shaggy-thighed wood that no one could ever find it. She could not think upon that ultimate possibility. As always, at this time, she knew with the Bible-black certainty of prayer that here was the place. Here nothing would be denied her.

The boxes and packages she kept locked in the car trunk. These were things she bought on impulse during her lunch hour or on Saturday, as though each purchase were for herself. She had not thought there were so many, but the oblong, white boxes and the largest flat box—all of them—seemed to leap into her arms. Without pausing she ran across a culvert and across a flat small meadow and into the first sentinel trees at the oak grove's edge.

Too late she realized the briers also guarded the grove. They had grown and had become heavy as barbed wire since the last time.

With the white boxes held high above her head, and with her robe open, flapping behind her, she leaped high and for a moment seemed to float above the caress of briers. She landed running. Her legs burned. But Miss Festner did not cry out.

Ahead she saw the smooth arena, in the center of her secret grove of oaks.

"Here, oh here," she said to the briers, which seemed to roll away in unbroken humps of light toward a creek beyond.

"Here. I am here, now," she said to the crossed branches of the trees overhead. "Here . . ."

She took off her robe.

She spread the robe near the boxes, at the edge of the clearing. Carefully in the moonlight she searched the clay ground, inch by inch; there was no dung, and no hair of cattle wedged in the bark of the oak trees. As she had imagined as she drove those limestone roads, the grove was clean, clean.

In the middle of the hoof-packed clay in the center of the grove of oaks, Miss Festner lay herself down upon the ground, which now seemed warm under the muscles of her flesh.

Nothing did come to her.

She was alone.

She listened but she heard only the mockery of silence among the trunks of trees. The intricate thunder of possibility shook her: was this the end, was she to be deserted like this at the final meeting place between two hills?

Then she heard it cough.

Nearby in the encircling brier she heard its jaws nibble the harsh vegetation. A small branch ripped under the plunge of a hoof. Then she heard it above her, high in the canopy of branches overhead;

perhaps it was now looking down at the raised, white supplication of her arms.

She heard once more the cry of the loon: near, then far away. She heard something hoarse, and very close, in the ring of the briers. Held fast in the bondage of her desire, she lay with eyes closed in the moonlight, and still nothing came to her.

Over, she thought. Oh over and gone and never again to return to me. She realized a truth about herself: since the first time when the hair was sweet as a cloud of wool above her she had given more and more of herself. She had walked much, had driven farther and farther into strange woods. Then, like a reprieve, the coarse odor came to her. The lust of its eye rustled the briers.

The gifts. Yes, the boxes piled near her robe. Each time, with gifts, she also gave more and more. At first it was only a flower tossed lightly upon the sand bar. Then her gifts were only the green enticement, but finally she had to give the silks of reward, everything. . . .

In a frenzy she opened her gifts.

Against rocks she broke the expensive, sullen perfumes. Each vial shattered and split and this enticement by odor overwhelmed even the trunks of the black trees.

Oh, come to me?

She paused, listened.

Somewhere beyond the shadows, somewhere in the forest of that night she felt something advance. She felt something come closer to her.

Her quick money-counting fingers clawed at the smaller boxes. She ripped tissue paper from all the jewels she had purchased at all the big jewelry stores all across the city. Tiaras and small rings and pearls in white strands, all these she tore into shreds of diamonds and single rubies and broken pearls, and these she threw into the encircling briers.

Oh, come to me?

The odor—so lurid, so near—seemed to stroke her thighs, and then in the old way it seemed to retreat beyond her farthest gifts.

Without her seeming to touch the hoof-packed clay she ran to the largest, final package. This she had saved, for the habit of frugality could also be with her, even in moments of extravagance.

She opened the box. The white, intense fleece of a lamb was what she held aloft. She waved the fleece in the light of the clearing. She held the fleece above her lowing mouth. She allowed the fleece to fall like a shower of myrrh and spice, to fall like the color of flowers around her, to cover her shoulders and her back with the incense of new wool.

Oh, come to me?

When nothing came to her, Miss Festner ran toward the thing she heard, toward a harsh plunging noise, in those final briers.

But she stopped. She knew it had deceived her, and therefore she stood weeping and ruined, fanned by the hot cry of the loon, in the center of briers and all her nights.

III

Escrow, Checking, Loans, and finally a Teller's cage: she had worked through each department, and now as the green floodgate doors of the bank opened, promptly at ten, she watched people swim into the bright hard marble pool of light, the interior of First National, Main.

In the hard security of a Teller's cage, she began this day by loosening the green drawstrings of green moneybags. Rolls of coins were what she found in each puffy little sack, rolls of dimes, and quarters, and half dollars, each roll made especially for her hand. In even rows the packets of bills, the twenties and fifties, fit precisely into each slot of her tray, and she felt the first smile of the morning hazard its first trial with the flesh of her own lips and cheeks as a customer snuffled just beyond the bars of her window.

From up the line, from Window Number One, Miss Festner heard the money-counting sound of laughter. The sound of the laughter made her see the two derby hats and the two false beards of the two men who were shaking hands with a Vice-President in the officers' enclosure, across the room. When she also saw the two beards rise and fall with the handshakes of the two men, she felt her own mouth pick up the laughter and pass it on to the next Teller in the long, money-counting line.

The State's Centennial Year, it was. The State Banking Inspectors were making believe. Across the room, in the officers' marble enclosure, two short men in make-believe beards began to laugh and laugh.

While her fingers counted out sixty-nine-sixty of a pensioner's check, which had snuffled under the bars of her window, she knew the ledgers and the adding machine tapes folded and held with paper clips and the dormant accounts and the Escrows were writhing, somewhere in the vaults or the storage rooms of First National, Main Branch.

Though the bills and the coins flowed through and around and over her fingers as water flows over and around a sand bar in some moonlit creek, the two derby hats and the beards of false gray hair seemed to float, seemed to become an echo, in the high corners of the main floor.

The edges of marble, the parallel shadows on the foot-trampled floor, the parallel lines of the brass-barred window before her, were the squares and the bars of a place she clearly remembered.

Across the bridge, beyond the village edge, was where the pens were. There in Ohio, beyond the edge of a limestone road, she had awakened from the sleepless dawns of girlhood to hear the cruel roosters cry *blood, blood, bloooood* across the sties and pens and across the hen yard's dusty wallows. Often she lay in her bed, listening to the sounds of animals already awake; the snigger of boars or somewhere in the corner of a pasture the dry dirt-pawing hoof of her father's bull. The dirt, the droppings of turkeys and pea fowl, and the dung of sparrows on a beam under the barn's eave were always there, or were seen in memory only as a brown composite of wind and random dust flapping across barnyards.

In that house the women swept floors, brushed crumbs from tables, rocked toward evening, waited for the odor of farm boots and the odor of work clothes, denim jackets, and old felt hats to walk through kitchen doors; waited until the warm odor of milk drifted into the fried heat of a kitchen in March

In summer a tomcat lolled on the tendrils and the matted leaves of a grape arbor, and stared all day at the martin's box high on a curved, white pole.

Mostly she remembered the things maimed: a rabbit leaping from stubble into the light of her father's sickle bar; the cut-shoat's lyric scream; the pullet, headless toward noon, butting a post of her mother's clothesline. Or the hired men, their fingers aligned at the thresher's dinner table, each man with something clipped off, missing: a finger gone to the nibbling belt of a corn sheller, a toe left at a chopping block, a hand or a forearm shucked by the whirling, frost-wet picker rolls.

All of that was past. She had gone to school, though she had visited her old home out of sentiment at the change of each season. For three years she taught at a consolidated high school. Though she tried to beat them with a yardstick the hulking baseball and football and basketball players refused to obey her. Finally the principal said why after all the First National, Main, paid twice as much, and then she could really have a place of her own. Therefore she had gone to live at the edge of this town, where sometimes a goat coughed in the catalpa leaves, and the backward curve of horn was mother-of-pearl in the moist light of the moon.

The two Inspectors came back toward noon.

Finally they began to work. Because it really was the Centennial Year, they wore derby hats and gray, false whiskers while they walked in and out of the officers' marble enclosure, or in and out of the vaults. She heard them laughing as they worked, and from her window it seemed they walked through the glass partitions. Toward three o'clock they walked past, together, nibbling a candy bar with their white goat teeth; and then they were behind the row of Tellers, nibbling stacks and stacks of twenties and fifties with their money-counting fingers.

At four o'clock doors were locked and the blinds were drawn, and only the feet and the knees of people walked past in the disembodied street. When she saw the legs walking past, Miss Festner thought, Why yes, tomorrow or the next day some one of the officers will walk up behind me and will stare and will then walk away as though he had seen something different. Then she would say what she knew all the others like her always said to the press: For my friends, for my friends, I did it, because I wanted them to be as happy as I have always been. You see, I gave it all to my friends . . .

At check-out, in the steel-lined vault, she saw the other money trays, all in a row. She knew this might be her last night at home in her own bed, in the room where the catalpa leaves were sometimes perfume in the night.

For the last time, tonight, she knew she might hear the hoofs firm upon the lowest branches, might see the flanks slender, stretched upward among the leaves, and might see also that final, unwinking eye stare at her from the tenderness of leaves.

Without hesitation she opened her massive, over-the-shoulder purse. Into the wide unlatched maw she stuffed all the singles and bundles of twenties and bundles of fifty dollar bills that her country hands could gather. In case, oh, in case it was money that was wanted, after all.

As always, Mr. Nelscot was standing at the bank door.

He smiled and he bowed very slightly as he let Miss Festner and her valise of a purse out the door.

All over again she heard the click of the door of First National, Main, behind her. She knew he would never do more than smile, would never do more than bow ever so slightly as he opened the door for her to leave. Or had that been his voice, after all; had he said as she left, as the door shut and clicked somewhere in the past and also in the future of her days, had he said too late, "See you. Same time tomorrow?"

MARK COSTELLO

MURPHY'S XMAS

The term experimental *has been used to justify bales and bales of sloppy, shoddy, careless work committed by those who would like to be writers without submitting to the difficulties of their craft. Here, though, the much-abused term can be honorably applied. Here we find the sort of innovations brought into the art of fiction by Joyce and Faulkner—a writer with something important to tell us has modified the conventions of syntax and typography in a search for means to revitalize them and make them fully responsible to his perception of the truth in experience.*

Note particularly how several paragraphs break off and new paragraphs resume in the middle of sentences. Note how Annie's dialogue in her phone conversation with Murphy is transformed from what she probably said into what he probably heard while she spoke. Note how consistently shifts from the expected language to the unexpected represent the skips in Murphy's frantic emotions—how Lincoln's coffin becomes Mrs. Murphy's womb, and so on.

Murphy's drunk on the bright verge of still another Christmas and a car door slams. Then he's out in the headlights and in bed waking up the next afternoon with Annie kissing his crucified right fist. It's blue and swollen, and when he tries to move it, it tingles, it chimes and Annie says, How did you hurt your hand? Did you hit somebody?

Murphy waits while that question fades on her mouth, then the

room glitters and he sniffs the old fractured acid of remorse asking:
Was I sick?

Yes.

Where?

On the floor. And you fell out of bed twice. It was so terrible I
don't think I could stand it if it happened again promise me you
won't get drunk anymore, Glover had to teach both of your classes
this morning you frighten me when you're this way and you've lost
so much weight you should have seen yourself last night lying naked
on the floor like something from a concentration camp in your own
vomit you were so white you were *blue*

is the color of Annie's eyes as Murphy sinks into the stars and
splinters of the sheets with her, making love to her and begging her
forgiveness which she gives and gives until Murphy can feel her shy
skeleton waltzing away with his in a fit of ribbons, the bursting
bouquets of a Christmas they are going to spend apart and

bright the next morning they rise in sweet sorrow to part for
Christmas; she to her parents' home in Missouri, he to haunted
Illinois.

Murphy holds her head in his hands and whispers: I can't leave
you. I won't be able to sleep. I know I won't. I'll get sick. I need you
Annie.

She squeezes his shoulders, kisses his cheeks and tells him he can
do it. It's only for two weeks. Good-bye. And be careful. Driving.

The door slams, the windows rattle and Annie walking through
the snow is no bigger than her cello which she holds to her shoulder,
a suitcase bangs against her left knee and the door opens and there's
Glover jangling the keys of his Volkswagen, offering again to drive
Murphy's family into Illinois for him.

Stricken by swerving visions of his son strewn across the wet
December roadside, his toys and intestines glistening under the
wheels of semi trucks, Murphy says no, he will drive and as he takes
the proffered keys, Glover says: Is Annie gone already? I was
supposed to give her a cello lesson before she left

then he leaves, the door slams and Murphy hates him, his
Byronesque limp through the snow, his cello and his Volkswagen
and sobriety. Rubbing his right fist, Murphy goes to the kitchen

and drains a can of beer. Then he packs his bag and lights out for his abandoned home.

II

Now the trunks are tied down and the Volkswagen is overladen and they roll out of Kansas into Missouri with the big wind knocking them all over the road while vigilant Murphy fights the wheel and grins at the feather touches of his 5-year-old son, who kisses his neck and romps in the back seat, ready for Christmas.

In Mexico, Missouri, his wife looks at his swollen right fist and says: Tsk-tsk. You haven't grown up yet have you. Who did you hit this time?

Into the face of her challenge, Murphy blows blue cigarette smoke.

When they cross the Mighty Mississippi at Hannibal, she looks up at the old, well-kept houses, pats her swollen stomach and says: Maybe I could come here to live, to have my baby.

Murphy's son rushes into the crack of her voice. And he doesn't stop asking him to come back and be his daddy again until Murphy takes Dexamyl to keep awake and it is dark and his son is asleep and the Volkswagen hops and shudders over the flat mauve stretches of Illinois.

At Springfield, where they stop to take on gas, the fluorescent light of the filling station is like the clap of a blue hand across the face. Murphy's son wakes and his wife says: This is where President Lincoln lived and is buried.

Where?

In a tomb. Out there.

She points a finger past his nose and Murphy makes a promise he knows he can't keep: I know what. Do you want to hear a poem, Michael?

With his son at the back of his neck all snug in a car that he should never have presumed to borrow, he drives through Springfield trying to remember "When Lilacs Last in the Dooryard

Bloom'd." But he can't get past the first stanza. Three times he repeats "O powerful western fallen star," and then goes on in prose about the coffin moving across the country with the pomp of the inloop'd flags, through cities draped in black until his son is asleep again and

that coffin becomes his wife's womb and from deep in its copious satin Murphy hears the shy warble of the fetus: *you are my father, you are my father,* the throat bleeds, the song bubbles. Murphy is afraid enough to fight. He looks at his wife and remembers the wily sunlight of conception, the last time he made love to her amid the lace iron and miniature American flags of the Veterans Cemetery (it's the quietest place I know to talk, she said) while the crows slipped across the sun like blue razor blades and the chatter of their divorce sprang up around them

stone and pine, lilac and star, the cedars dusk and dim: *well it's final then, we're definitely going to get a divorce?* Murphy said *yes,* for good? *yes* and his wife caught him by the hip as he turned away *well it's almost dark now so why don't we just lie down and fuck once more for old time's sake here on the grass come on there are pine needles and they're soft*

Did you take your pill?

Yes

Ok, but no strings attached and

3½ months later Murphy is informed that he is going to be a father again and again, hurray, whoopee now

Murphy drives across slippery Illinois hearing a carol of death until the singer so shy becomes a child he will never hold or know, and the sweet chant of its breath gets caught in the whine of the tires as he imagines holding the child and naming it and kissing it, until it falls asleep on his shoulder—*how could you have tricked me this way? how could you have done it?*

That question keeps exploding behind Murphy's eyes, and when they hit his wife's hometown, he stops the car in front of a tavern and says: I can't do it.

What?

Face your parents.

He gets out: I'll wait here. Come back when you're unloaded.

His wife says *wait a minute,* and Murphy slams the door. He walks under the glittering Budweiser sign and she screams: I can't drive. I don't even know how to get this thing in reverse . . .

Push down.

Child!

Murphy hovers over the car: *I'm not a child!* and the motor roars, and the gears grind, and the Volkswagen hops and is dead. A red light flashes on in the middle of the speedometer and Murphy turns to the wakening face of 5-year-old Michael: Are we at Grandma's yet Daddy?

He slams his swollen right fist into his left palm: Yes we are!

Then he gets in and takes the wheel. And he drives them all the way home.

But he doesn't stop there. Murphy roars northwest out of Illinois into Iowa in search of friends and gin he can't find. Then he bangs back across the Mississippi, cuts down the heart of Illinois, and holes up in the YMCA in his wife's hometown, within visiting distance of his son.

Whom he loves and doesn't see. He keeps telling himself: *I think I'll surprise Michael and take him to the park this afternoon,* then he races down to the gym to run in circles and spit against the walls. He sits in the steam room, watches the clock and slaps his stomach, which is flat, but on the blink. To ease his pain, he drinks milk and eats cottage cheese and yogurt and calls Annie long distance in Missouri: God I love you and miss your body Annie I haven't slept for two days

and she says: Guess what?

What?

Glover was through town and gave me a cello lesson, he's a great guy his

gifts are stunning and relentless, he limps off to take your classes when you're too drunk to stand up in the morning—his hair is scrubbed, his skin cherubic, his wrists are opal and delicate; right now Murphy would like to sieze them and break them off. Instead he says: Is he still in town?

Who?

Glover

Heavens no, he just stopped through for about two hours are you all right?

Yes. Listen Annie I love you

Murphy slams the phone down and bounds back upstairs to his room in the YMCA to sit alone while his cottage cheese and yogurt cartons fill up with snow on the window ledge and he imagines Annie back in their rooms in Kansas. When she walks across the floor her heels ring against the walls and every morning Murphy hears her before he sees her standing at the stove, her hair dark, her earrings silver, her robe wine, her thighs so cool, and the pearl flick of her tongue is like a beak when she kisses him

Murphy tastes unbelievable mint and blood and

imagines Glover limping across the floor of the living room with two glasses of gin in his hands. The betrayal is dazzling and quick. Bending under Glover's tongue, Annie whispers *no, no,* and as she goes down in their bed, her fingers make star-shaped wrinkles in the sheets

Murphy slams his fist down on his YMCA windowsill. Then popping them like white bullwhips over his head, he stuffs his towels and clothes into his bag, and lights out of there on lustrous Highway 47. The night is prodigal, the inane angels of the radio squawk out their thousand songs of Christmas and return. Bearing down on the wheel, Murphy murders the memory of Annie and Glover with the memory of his father, whom he has betrayed to old age, the stars and stripes of the U.S. Mail.

Composing them on the back of his American Legion 40 *and* 8 stationery, Murphy's father sends quick notes By Air to his grandson saying: I was feeling pretty low x until I got the pictures you drew for me Michael boy x then I bucked up x God bless you x I miss you x give my love to your daddy x who

unblessed and rocking in the slick crescents of Dexamyl and fatigue, is on his way home for still another Christmas. Now as he drives, he notes the dim absence of birds on the telephone lines, and thinking of the happy crows that Michael draws with smiles in their beaks, Murphy sees his father stumbling under the sign of the cross, crossing himself again and again on the forehead and lips, crossing himself on his tie clasp, wandering in a listless daze across the front lawn with a rake in his hands, not knowing whether to clean the gutter along the street or pray for his own son, who has sunk so low out in Kansas.

It is just dawning when Murphy breaks into the mauve and white outskirts of his dear dirty Decatur where billboards and *Newport* girls in turquoise are crowned by the bursting golden crosses of Murphy's high school then

he's home. Pulled up and stopped in his own driveway. And sitting there with his hands crossed in his lap he feels agog like a Buddhistic time bomb about to go off, about to splinter and explode inside the dry sleep of his parents, the tears will smoulder, the braying angels of insomnia will shatter around the childless Christmas tree, there will be a fire, it will sputter and run up the walls and be Murphy's fault. Sitting there he feels hearts beginning to pump in the palms of his hands and he doesn't want to let anybody die

as he knocks on the dry oaken door of his parents' home and is welcomed with open arms and the sun rising behind his back

Inside the sockets of his mother's eyes, there are mauve circles and they have had the living room walls painted turquoise. Murphy blinks, shakes his father's hand, and his mother leads him into the kitchen.

There he drinks milk, eats cottage cheese and kisses his mother's hands. She cries and wants him to eat a big breakfast. With tears in her eyes, she offers him bacon, eggs, cornbread, coffee, butterchunk sweet rolls and Brazil nuts. When Murphy shakes his head she says: I think you're making the biggest mistake of your life, I think you'll live to regret it. Patricia is a lovely girl, you have a wonderful son and another child on the way. Isn't there any hope of you getting back together? I pray night and day and can't get little Michael off my mind. What's ever going to happen to him and the new child? Oh I wish I were twenty years younger

After breakfast they go shopping, and for his Christmas present Murphy picks out three packs of stainless steel razor blades and a pair of black oxford basketball shoes. Then he slips off for a workout at his high school gym. The basketball team is practicing and Murphy runs in wide circles around them, not bothering a soul.

Left to himself that afternoon, he drinks rum and eggnog and plays with the remote controls of the color television set. Then he roams the house and neighborhood and everything has changed. The sheets of his bed are blue. On the walls, where once there were newspaper photographs of himself in high school basketball uniform, there are now purple paintings of Jesus Christ kneeling on rocks in the Garden of Gethsemane. Every place he looks, in corniced frames of diminishing size, there are color photographs of Murphy in tight-collared military attire. As he looks, the photographs get smaller and smaller and there is always a snub-nosed statue of St. Francis of Assisi standing there, to measure himself by.

Up and down the block, birds bang in and out of bird feeders. The withering neighbors have put up fences within fences within fences. Half-drunk, Murphy keeps hitting the wrong switches and floodlights glare from the roof of the garage and light up the whole backyard. All night long his father keeps paying the encroaching negro carolers not to sing. Finally Murphy gets up from the sofa, and smiling, announces that he's going out. Taking his rum and eggnog with him, he sits in the Volkswagen and drinks until 3 o'clock in the morning. Then he gets out, vomits on the curb and goes back inside

Where his mother is awake in a nightgown of shriveled violet, with yellow spears of wheat sewn into the shoulders like cross-staves of static lightning about to go off and how

will Murphy hold her when she stops him on the carpet outside his bedroom door to tell him that she loves him, that he will always be her son no matter what happens she is so sorry that he had to leave his wife and children for

a mere girl, it is unbelievable that

in his hands her small skull buzzes and even before she mentions the fact of Annie, Murphy is holding Annie's skull in his hands and the sinking wings of his mother's sweet shoulders are Annie's shoulders in his mother's nightgown sinking: What are you talking about?

That girl you're living with. She called tonight

on Christmas Eve

Murphy hears the old familiar bells of his father's fury gonging

Your father answered, he was furious

Mother I'm not living with anyone

Michael I know you are

then the small lightning of her nightgown begins to strike across her shoulders and she is sobbing against his throat and Murphy is in bed holding his lie like a sheet up to his chin: Mother I told you I'm not living with anyone

Stroking his leg through the blankets, she disregards the crocked insomnia of his eyes, and makes him promise to try to sleep: Do you promise now?

Yes Mother, I promise

and she leaves him sleepless between the blue sheets with Christ kneeling on the wall, the scent of his mother's handcream on the back of his neck and he hears her alone in her room coughing like a wife he has lost at last and picking at her rosary beads all night long

There is no sleep

or peace on earth. But with the muzzy dawn Murphy rises and goes to church with his parents. In the choir loft, the organs shudder; in his pew Murphy shivers and sniffs the contrition of Christmastide. All around him the faithful kneel in candle smoke and pray; all day long Murphy kneels and shuffles around trying to get Annie *long distance,* trying to tell her *never to call him at home again.* Then at 7 P.M. the phone rings and Murphy's simmering 70-year-old father answers it hissing: Long distance, for you

By the time Murphy hangs up, his father is dizzy. He staggers through the rooms slamming doors while Murphy's mother follows him whispering: Mike your blood pressure, your blood pressure

Then in the living room they face each other: The bitch! Calling here on Christmas Day! The little bitch!

Murphy turns to his mother and says, *I'm leaving* and his father spins him by the shoulder: You're not leaving, *I* am!

They both leave. Murphy by the back, his father by the front. Storm doors slam, crucifixes rattle on the walls. Murphy's father rounds the corner and screams: Come back here!

His voice is higher than Murphy has ever heard it, and the wind pulls at their clothes while they walk toward each other, his father in a slanting stagger, his overcoat too big for him, his eyes filled with tears.

I'm an old man. I'm dying. You won't see me again. Go back to your family, don't abandon your son.

Murphy reaches for his shoulder and says *Dad I can't* and his father slaps his hand away

Michael Murphy. You have a son named *Michael Murphy* and you tell me you can't go back to him?

Murphy lifts his hand and starts to speak, but his father screams: *Phony!* You're a phon*eee*, do you hear me?

They are at the door and Murphy's mother, in grief and her nightgown, pulls them in. His father stumbles to the wall and hits it: You phony. You ought to be in Vietnam!

Murphy's laughter is curdled and relieved. He slaps his hands together and screams: That's it, that's it!

Then he spins and bolts toward the back door, with his mother screaming: Michael! Where are you going?

To Vietnam, god damn it! To Vietnam

Which isn't far. 150 miles north. From a motel room deep in her own hometown, Murphy calls his wife and when he asks her to come over she says: Why *should* I come over?

You know why. I'm going out of my mind.

Be my guest.

Click

She opens the door during half-time of a TV football game and neither of them says a word as their clothes fly in slurred arcs onto the bed. Then standing naked in front of her, Murphy hunches up with holy quietude and smiles and breathes as he holds a glass of gin and tonic to her lips and she drinks and smiles as the lime skin nudges her teeth and she nods when she's had enough. While her mouth is still cool, Murphy kisses her tongue and gums and wants to push the bed against the wall and then to drive all the other guests to insomniac rack and ruin by humping and banging the bed with wet good health against the wall all afternoon but

his wife is sunk in an older despair. She runs her fingers up the vapid stack of Murphy's spine and says: You *are* handsome. I love to touch you.

Bare-chested Murphy turns on it, and the quick trick of her flattery gets them into bed, where to the pelvic thud of the innerspring she sucks on the spare skin of his collarbone and says: Tell me that you love me. You don't have to mean it. Just say it . . .

Murphy would like to but he can't. Both memory and flesh legislate against him. He looks down, and like painted furniture his wife's ribs now seem chipped by a thousand kicks; when he takes them in his mouth, her nipples taste as tight and deprived as walnuts; within the pregnant strop of her stomach against his, Murphy can feel the delicate strophes of Annie's waist, and moving like a pale liar before his wife's bared teeth, he remembers the beginning of the end of their marriage; the masks, mirrors and carrots that began to sprout around their bed like a bitter, 2 A.M. Victory garden, one that Murphy had planted all by himself and was going to pick and shake in his wife's face on the sparkling, sacrosanct morning that he left for good and ever. Caught in the dowdy mosaics of their bedroom mirror, they would get down on their hands and knees and as the orange joke of a carrot disappeared between her legs, his wife would turn and ask, *who are you?* and Murphy would smile down from behind his mask and say: *who are you?* Then his smile would rot in his opened mouth, and Murphy *became* his impersonations; he played and moaned within an adultery so hypothetical it stunk and smoked the bedroom ceiling up like the induced death of love between them *Harder, Oh Harder* now Murphy and his father are standing outside the motel room window looking in at Murphy's marriage like peeping toms and his father is ordering Murphy back into the bed but Murphy resists and all of his reasons are rosy and shrill like a schoolboy he screams: *I wouldn't swap Annie for anybody, do you hear me, not anybody* and his father, in tears and death, screams: *Not for your son? Not for Michael Murphy? i'm*

Coming

and Murphy opens his eyes to endure his wife's orgasm like a slap across the face *Oh Thank You God, Oh Thank You.*

Thanking her with whispers and pecks about the neck and ears, Murphy sweeps his wife out into the brittle December afternoon and bright the next morning he picks up his son to take him home, 150 miles south, to his grandmother. Michael's raucous teeth glitter in the rearview mirror of the VW, and as they rattle into Decatur, Murphy loves him so much, he can't stop or share him with anybody just yet: I know what Michael. Do you want to go to the zoo before we go to Grandma's? Yes

he does. Right now. And Murphy, full of grins and flapdoodle, takes him there. He buys Michael a bag of popcorn, and as he goes back to the car to flick off the headlights, he turns to see the popcorn falling in white, jerky sprays among the ducks and geese.

The whole pause at the zoo is that way: spendthrift, inaugural and loving. Murphy squats and shows Michael how to feed the steaming billy goat with his bare hands. He flinches and giggles at the pink pluck of his lips, then they race over to look through the windows at the pacing leopards. Bare-handed and standing there, Murphy wonders how he would defend his son against a leopard. He can feel his fists and forearms being ripped away, but also he can feel his son escaping into the dusk and dim of the elm trees that surround the zoo.

Then he gets zany and amid giggles and protests, Murphy drives the borrowed VW up over the curb and through the park to Grandmother's house they go with the radio blaring: help I need somebody's help then

suddenly its darker and cooler and their smiles are whiter when the subject changes like a slap across the face to

Michael's dreams. Five years old in a fatherless house, he sleeps alone and dreams of snow. Murphy pulls him into the front seat, sets him on his lap and turns off the radio. Holding him too tight, he says: what kind of snow Michael?

You know. The kind that falls.

What do you dream?

That it's covering me up.

Then Michael begins to cry and says: I want somebody to sleep with me tonight and tomorrow night. I want *you* to sleep with me Daddy.

Murphy does. Three nights they stay in his parents' house and Murphy sleeps between the blue sheets while Michael sucks his thumb and urinates the first night against Murphy's leg, giving him the chance to be patient father loving his son

he carries him to the bathroom with sure avowals and tender kisses: That's all right Michael boy, Dad will take care of you

Always?

Always

and Murphy's mother is there in her nightgown in the stark light of the bedroom changing the sheets, putting down towels, kissing her grandson, wishing she were twenty years younger

In the lilac morning, quick with clouds and sunlight, Murphy and his mother and son go uptown. Standing in front of laughing mirrors in the Buster Brown Shoe Store, Murphy and Michael grow fat and skinny and tall and short together, then go to see Pinnochio not in the belly of a whale

but in the outer space of sure death and forgiveness, they eat silver sno-cones and Murphy is finally able to eat steak while his father roams through the rooms presenting his grandson with a plastic pistol on the barrel of which an assassin's scope has been mounted.

Compounding that armament with love, he displays, on the last afternoon, Murphy's basketball clippings. Spreading them out for his grandson on the bed, he whispers, smiles and gloats until 5-year-old Michael can't help himself. He walks over to Murphy and says: Grandpa says you were a great basketball player and played on TV is that right Daddy?

That's right Michael, then they

are leaving. Clasping his toys to him, Michael cries pained and formal tears. Murphy stands on the curb, the wind in his eyes, and the apologies are yet to be made. Overhead the streetlight clangs and they are standing on the same corner where Murphy used to sit under the streetlight at night on the orange fire hydrant twirling his rosary beads like a black propeller over his head waiting for his parents to come home and light up the dark rooms with their voices and cigarettes then

he would see their headlights coming up the street and he would rise and put away his rosary beads to greet them now

he takes off his gloves and puts out his right hand to his father and says: Dad, I'm sorry.

When his apology cracks the air, his mother begins to cry. Grateful for that cue, his father takes his hand and says Good-bye, good luck, God bless you

III

Out there in Kansas the next afternoon, under a sere and benedictory sun, Murphy's Christmas comes to an end. He tools west away from home and the holidays, southwest toward the snaggled conclusion of still another New Year. His family rides in a swarm of shredded Kleenex, Cracker Jack, and terror referred

is terror refined: like the crucial envoy of his grandfather, Michael, sweet assassin, holds his plastic pistol to the base of Murphy's skull and says: Daddy? Why don't you come back and be my daddy?

Terse and perspirate, Murphy's wife takes a swipe at the pistol, but Michael moves out of her reach, and keeping it trained on the back of his father's skull, he repeats his question: Why don't you come back Daddy?

Before he can think or excuse himself, Murphy says, *Because.*

Because why?

Because Mommy and I fight.

You're not fighting now.

In tears and on her knees, Murphy's wife lunges into the back seat and disarms her son. But he begins to cry and find his ultimatum: Daddy

I'm too shy to have a new daddy, I want you to be my daddy, and if you won't come back and be my daddy

I'm going to kill you.

The moment of his threat is considered. And then it is foregone. Out of his fist and index finger, Michael makes a pistol and a patricide: Bang, bang, bang

you're dead Daddy

you're dead

Coffin that passes through lanes and streets, Volkswagen that blows and rattles under the new snow's perpetual clang, here, Murphy hands over his sprig of lilac and return, his modicum of rage and disbelief.

Certain that his son's aim was shy and hypothetical, he stops the Volkswagen in front of his apartment, flicks off the headlights, slams the door and hears the

dual squawk of tuned and funereal cellos

their notes curdle the snow, splinter the windows with a welcome so baroque and sepulchral, Murphy can't stand it. Roaring toward the door, he imagines Annie and Glover sitting on stiff-backed chairs, their cellos between their legs, their innocence arranged by Bach, certified by

the diagonal churn of their bows on string, the spiny octagons of their music stands, the opal bone and nylon of Annie's knees. Murphy rattles the door with his fist, and for a moment their music needles his rage, then squeaks to a stop. In turquoise slacks and sweater, with a smile brimful of tears and teeth so bright, Annie throws open the door and how

will Murphy return her kiss, while blurred in the corner of his eye, Glover scurries, gathering up his cello and his music: *Happy New Year did the car run all right* he takes the proffered keys and guilty of nothing but his embarrassment

he says *don't mention it* as he leaves, slams out the door, and

left in the rattled vacuum of that departure, Murphy has no one to beat up or murder, no one on whom to avenge his Christmas; he is left with only the echo of the music, a suspicion founded on nothing but a cherub's limp and hustle through the chiming snow.

In bed, Annie is a sweet new anatomy of hope and extinction. She kisses him, the *Newport* flood of her hair gets in his eyes and Murphy cracks an elegiac and necessary joke: *Annie you'll never leave me for Glover will you?* She tells him not to be silly then

Murphy kisses her, and in a rush of flesh and new avowals, he puts everything into his lovemaking but his

heart

which hangs unbelievable and dead in his ribs, all shot to smithereens by Michael.

Outside the new snow falls and inside it is over. Annie is asleep in his arms and Murphy lies sleepless on a numb and chiming cross of his own making. On the walls there are no praying Christs, the turquoise Gethsemanes of Decatur are gone forever. The clock drones, the womb whirs, the shy trill of his wife's gestation comes to Murphy through the pines like Michael calling to him: *Sleep with me tonight and tomorrow night Daddy* the cradle's eloquence depends on pain, it is sewn in lilacs and shocks of wheat. Shy charlatan, Murphy sneaks up to it and in a room full of white, white sunlight, he looks in at his newborn child, and cannot look away or kid himself, his fatherhood is the fatherhood

of cottage cheese, the retreating footprints of snow and yogurt up his father's spine, the borrowed Volkswagen that will never run out of gas or plastic pistols. Then the dry bells of the furnace begin to hiss against Murphy's ankles, and he hears the whistling pines, the clangorous tombstones of the Veterans Cemetery. Flapping their arms like downed angels in the middle of winter, Murphy and Annie make love and forgive each other until their ears and eyesockets fill up with snow

then Michael stands over them, takes aim at Murphy and
makes his final declaration: Bang
bang, bang
you're dead Daddy
you're dead

IV

And for the first time in his life, Murphy lies there and knows it.

showing you what going on,
& you drew your own conclusion

half scien
a quarter scien

RICHARD YATES

THE BEST OF EVERYTHING

This story is straightforwardly realistic in approach. There are no distorting tricks of language. The presentation is essentially objective—that is, the author supplies very little interpretation.

The point of view shifts from one major character to the other and then back again. First we see everything as Grace witnessed it—then as Ralph did—then, again, as Grace did.

The heartbroken tone emerges more from the design of the plot and the incongruity of the characters forced together than from any devices of style. The irony arises from the events, and the author makes no judgment about right or wrong.

The story contains a classic example of a flashback executed with consummate skill and handsomely placed in the framework of the present action.

The climax of the story occurs when Grace asks Ralph to stay with her. His crudely inadequate response to her invitation represents the resolution of the action and completes the statement of the story's theme.

give you a lot of information

Nobody expected Grace to do any work the Friday before her wedding. In fact, nobody would let her, whether she wanted to or not.

A gardenia corsage lay in a cellophane box beside her typewriter —from Mr. Atwood, her boss—and tucked inside the envelope that came with it was a ten-dollar gift certificate from Bloomingdale's. Mr. Atwood had treated her with a special shy courtliness ever since the time she necked with him at the office Christmas party, and now when she went in to thank him he was all hunched over, rattling desk drawers, blushing and grinning and barely meeting her eyes.

"Aw, now, don't mention it, Grace," he said. "Pleasure's all mine. Here, you need a pin to put that gadget on with?"

"There's a pin that came with it," she said, holding up the corsage. "See? A nice white one."

Beaming, he watched her pin the flowers high on the lapel of her suit. Then he cleared his throat importantly and pulled out the writing panel of his desk, ready to give the morning's dictation. But it turned out there were only two short letters, and it wasn't until an hour later, when she caught him handing over a pile of dictaphone cylinders to Central Typing, that she realized he had done her a favor.

"That's very sweet of you, Mr. Atwood," she said, "but I do think you ought to give me all your work today, just like any oth—"

"Aw, now, Grace," he said. "You only get married once."

The girls all made a fuss over her too, crowding around her desk and giggling, asking again and again to see Ralph's photograph ("Oh, he's *cute!*"), while the office manager looked on nervously, reluctant to be a spoilsport but anxious to point out that it was, after all, a working day.

Then at lunch there was the traditional little party at Schrafft's —nine women and girls, giddy on their unfamiliar cocktails, letting their chicken à la king grow cold while they pummeled her with old times and good wishes. There were more flowers and another gift—a silver candy dish for which all the girls had whisperingly chipped in.

Grace said "Thank you" and "I certainly do appreciate it" and "I don't know what to say" until her head rang with the words and the corners of her mouth ached from smiling, and she thought the afternoon would never end.

Ralph called up about four o'clock, exuberant. "How ya doin', honey?" he asked, and before she could answer he said, "Listen. Guess what I got?"

"I don't know. A present or something? What?" She tried to sound excited, but it wasn't easy.

"A bonus. Fifty dollars." She could almost see the flattening of his lips as he said "fifty dollars" with the particular earnestness he reserved for pronouncing sums of money.

"Why, that's lovely, Ralph," she said, and if there was any tiredness in her voice he didn't notice it.

"Lovely, huh?" he said with a laugh, mocking the girlishness of the word. "Ya *like* that, huh Gracie? No, but I mean I was really surprised, ya know it? The boss siz, 'Here, Ralph,' and he hands me this envelope. He don't even crack a smile or nothin', and I'm wonderin', what's the deal here? I'm getting fired here, or what? He siz, 'G'ahead, Ralph, open it.' So I open it, and then I look at the boss and he's grinning a mile wide." He chuckled and sighed. "Well, so listen, honey. What time ya want me to come over tonight?"

"Oh, I don't know. Soon as you can, I guess."

"Well listen, I gotta go over to Eddie's house and pick up that bag he's gonna loan me, so I might as well do that, go on home and eat, and then come over to your place around eight-thirty, nine o'clock. Okay?"

"All right," she said. "I'll see you then, darling." She had been calling him "darling" for only a short time—since it had become irrevocably clear that she was, after all, going to marry him—and the word still had an alien sound. As she straightened the stacks of stationery in her desk (because there was nothing else to do), a familiar little panic gripped her: she couldn't marry him—she hardly even *knew* him. Sometimes it occurred to her differently, that she couldn't marry him because she knew him too well, and either way it left her badly shaken, vulnerable to all the things that Martha, her roommate, had said from the very beginning.

"Isn't he funny?" Martha had said after their first date. "He says 'terlet.' I didn't know people really said 'terlet.'" And Grace had giggled, ready enough to agree that it *was* funny. That was a time when she had been ready to agree with Martha on practically anything—when it often seemed, in fact, that finding a girl like Martha from an ad in the *Times* was just about the luckiest thing that had ever happened to her.

But Ralph had persisted all through the summer, and by fall she had begun standing up for him. "What don't you like about him, Martha? He's perfectly nice."

"Oh, everybody's perfectly nice, Grace," Martha would say in her college voice, making perfectly nice a faintly absurd thing to be, and then she'd look up crossly from the careful painting of her fingernails. "It's just that he's such a little—a little *white worm.* Can't you see that?"

"Well, I certainly don't see what his *complexion* has to do with—"

"Oh God, *you* know what I mean. Can't you see what I *mean?* Oh, and all those friends of his, his Eddie and his Marty and his George with their mean, ratty little clerks' lives and their mean, ratty little. . . . It's just that they're all *alike,* those people. All they ever say is 'Hey, wha' happen t'ya Giants?' and 'Hey, wha' happen t'ya Yankees?' and they all live way out in Sunnyside or Woodhaven or some awful place, and their mothers have those damn little china elephants on the mantelpiece." And Martha would frown over her nail polish again, making it clear that the subject was closed.

All that fall and winter she was confused. For a while she tried going out only with Martha's kind of men—the kind that used words like "amusing" all the time and wore small-shouldered flannel suits like a uniform; and for a while she tried going out with no men at all. She even tried that crazy business with Mr. Atwood at the office Christmas party. And all the time Ralph kept calling up, hanging around, waiting for her to make up her mind. Once she took him home to meet her parents in Pennsylvania (where she never would have dreamed of taking Martha), but it wasn't until Easter time that she finally gave in.

They had gone to a dance somewhere in Queens, one of the big American Legion dances that Ralph's crowd was always going to, and when the band played "Easter Parade" he held her very close, hardly moving, and sang to her in a faint, whispering tenor. It was the kind of thing she'd never have expected Ralph to do—a sweet, gentle thing—and it probably wasn't just then that she decided to marry him, but it always seemed so afterwards. It always seemed she had decided that minute, swaying to the music with his husky voice in her hair:

> *"I'll be all in clover*
> *And when they look you over*
> *I'll be the proudest fella*
> *In the Easter Parade. . . ."*

That night she had told Martha, and she could still see the look on Martha's face. "Oh, Grace, you're not—surely you're not *serious*. I mean, I thought he was more or less of a *joke*—you can't really mean you want to—"

"Shut up! You just shut up, Martha!" And she'd cried all night. Even now she hated Martha for it; even as she stared blindly at a row of filing cabinets along the office wall, half sick with fear that Martha was right.

The noise of giggles swept over her, and she saw with a start that [back to the office] two of the girls—Irene and Rose—were grinning over their typewriters and pointing at her. "*We* saw ya!" Irene sang. "*We* saw ya! Mooning again, huh Grace?" Then Rose did a burlesque of mooning, heaving her meager breasts and batting her eyes, and they both collapsed in laughter.

With an effort of will Grace resumed the guileless, open smile of a bride. The thing to do was concentrate on plans.

Tomorrow morning, "bright and early," as her mother would say, she would meet Ralph at Penn Station for the trip home. They'd arrive about one, and her parents would meet the train. "Good t'see ya, Ralph!" her father would say, and her mother would probably kiss him. A warm, homely love filled her: *they* wouldn't call him a white worm; *they* didn't have any ideas about Princeton men and "interesting" men and all the other kinds of men Martha was so stuck-up about. Then her father would probably take Ralph out for a beer and show him the paper mill where he worked (and at least Ralph wouldn't be snobby about a person working in a paper mill, either), and then Ralph's family and friends would come down from New York in the evening.

*full
seen*

She'd have time for a long talk with her mother that night, and the next morning, "bright and early" (her eyes stung at the thought of her mother's plain, happy face), they would start getting dressed for the wedding. Then the church and the ceremony, and then the reception (Would her father get drunk? Would Muriel Ketchel sulk about not being a bridesmaid?), and finally the train to Atlantic City, and the hotel. But from the hotel on she couldn't plan any more. A door would lock behind her and there would be a wild, fantastic silence, and nobody in all the world but Ralph to lead the way.

"Well, Grace," Mr. Atwood was saying, "I want to wish you every happiness." He was standing at her desk with his hat and coat on, and all around her were the chattering and scraping-back of chairs that meant it was five o'clock.

"Thank you, Mr. Atwood." She got to her feet, suddenly surrounded by all the girls in a bedlam of farewell.

"All the luck in the world, Grace."

"Drop us a card, huh Grace? From Atlantic City?"

"So long, Grace."

"G'night, Grace, and listen: the best of everything."

Finally she was free of them all, out of the elevator, out of the building, hurrying through the crowds to the subway.

When she got home Martha was standing in the door of the kitchenette, looking very svelte in a crisp new dress.

"Hi, Grace. I bet they ate you alive today, didn't they?"

"Oh no," Grace said. "Everybody was—real nice." She sat down, exhausted, and dropped the flowers and the wrapped candy dish on a table. Then she noticed that the whole apartment was swept and dusted, and the dinner was cooking in the kitchenette. "Gee, everything looks wonderful," she said. "What'd you do all this for?"

"Oh, well, I got home early anyway," Martha said. Then she smiled, and it was one of the few times Grace had ever seen her look shy. "I just thought it might be nice to have the place looking decent for a change, when Ralph comes over."

"Well," Grace said, "it certainly was nice of you."

The way Martha looked now was even more surprising: she looked awkward. She was turning a greasy spatula in her fingers, holding it delicately away from her dress and examining it, as if she had something difficult to say. "Look, Grace," she began. "You do understand why I can't come to the wedding, don't you?"

"Oh, sure." Grace said, although in fact she didn't, exactly. It was something about having to go up to Harvard to see her brother before he went into the Army, but it had sounded like a lie from the beginning.

"It's just that I'd hate you to think I—well, anyway, I'm glad if you do understand. And the other thing I wanted to say is more important."

"What?"

"Well, just that I'm sorry for all the awful things I used to say about Ralph. I never had a right to talk to you that way. He's a very sweet boy and I—well, I'm sorry, that's all."

It wasn't easy for Grace to hide a rush of gratitude and relief when she said, "Why, that's all right, Martha, I—"

"The chops are on fire!" Martha bolted for the kitchenette. "It's all right," she called back. "They're edible." And when she came out to serve dinner all her old composure was restored. "I'll have to eat and run," she said as they sat down. "My train leaves in forty minutes."

"I thought it was *tomorrow* you were going."

"Well, it was, actually," Martha said, "but I decided to go tonight. Because you see, Grace, another thing—if you can stand one more apology—another thing I'm sorry for is that I've hardly ever given you and Ralph a chance to be alone here. So tonight I'm going to clear out." She hesitated. "It'll be a sort of wedding gift from me, okay?" And then she smiled, not shyly this time but in a way that was more in character—the eyes subtly averted after a flicker of special meaning. It was a smile that Grace—through stages of suspicion, bewilderment, awe, and practiced imitation—had long ago come to associate with the word "sophisticated."

"Well, that's very sweet of you," Grace said, but she didn't really get the point just then. It wasn't until long after the meal was over and the dishes washed, until Martha had left for her train in a whirl of cosmetics and luggage and quick goodbyes, that she began to understand.

She took a deep, voluptuous bath and spent a long time drying herself, posing in the mirror, filled with a strange slow excitement. In her bedroom, from the rustling tissues of an expensive white box, she drew the prizes of her trousseau—a sheer nightgown of white nylon and a matching negligee—put them on, and went to the mirror again. She had never worn anything like this before, or felt like this, and the thought of letting Ralph see her like this sent her into the kitchenette for a glass of the special dry sherry Martha kept for cocktail parties. Then she turned out all the lights but one and, carrying her glass, went to the sofa and arranged herself there to wait for him. After a while she got up and brought the sherry bottle over to the coffee table, where she set it on a tray with another glass.

When Ralph left the office he felt vaguely let down. Somehow, he'd expected more of the Friday before his wedding. The bonus check had been all right (though secretly he'd been counting on twice that amount), and the boys had bought him a drink at lunch and kidded around in the appropriate way ("Ah, don't feel too bad, Ralph—worse things could happen"), but still, there ought to have been a real party. Not just the boys in the office, but Eddie, and *all* his friends. Instead there would only be meeting Eddie at the White Rose like every other night of the year, and riding home to borrow Eddie's suitcase and to eat, and then having to ride all the way back to Manhattan just to see Gracie for an hour or two. Eddie wasn't in the bar when he arrived, which sharpened the edge of his loneliness. Morosely he drank a beer, waiting.

Eddie was his best friend, and an ideal best man because he'd been in on the courtship of Gracie from the start. It was in this very bar, in fact, that Ralph had told him about their first date last summer: "Ooh, Eddie—what a paira *knockers!*"

And Eddie had grinned. "Yeah? So what's the roommate like?"

"Ah, you don't want the roommate, Eddie. The roommate's a dog. A snob, too, I think. No, but this *other* one, this little *Gracie*—boy, I mean, she is *stacked.*"

Half the fun of every date—even more than half—had been telling Eddie about it afterwards, exaggerating a little here and there, asking Eddie's advice on tactics. But after today, like so many other pleasures, it would all be left behind. Gracie had promised him at least one night off a week to spend with the boys, after they were married, but even so it would never be the same. Girls never understood a thing like friendship.

There was a ball game on the bar's television screen and he watched it idly, his throat swelling in a sentimental pain of loss. Nearly all his life had been devoted to the friendship of boys and men, to trying to be a good guy, and now the best of it was over.

Finally Eddie's stiff finger jabbed the seat of his pants in greeting. "Whaddya say, sport?"

Ralph narrowed his eyes to indolent contempt and slowly turned around. "Wha' happen ta you, wise guy? Get lost?"

"Whaddya—in a hurry a somethin'?" Eddie barely moved his lips when he spoke. "Can't wait two minutes?" He slouched on a stool and slid a quarter at the bartender. "Draw one, there, Jack."

They drank in silence for a while, staring at the television. "Got a little bonus today," Ralph said. "Fifty dollars."

"Yeah?" Eddie said. "Good."

A batter struck out; the inning was over and the commercial came on. "So?" Eddie said, rocking the beer around in his glass. "Still gonna get married?"

"Why not?" Ralph said with a shrug. "Listen, finish that, willya? I wanna get a move on."

"Wait awhile, wait awhile. What's ya hurry?"

"C'mon, willya?" Ralph stepped impatiently away from the bar. "I wanna go pick up ya bag."

"Ah, bag schmagg."

Ralph moved up close again and glowered at him. "Look, wise guy. Nobody's gonna *make* ya loan me the goddamn bag, ya know. I don't wanna break ya *heart* or nothin'—"

"Arright, arright, arright. You'll getcha bag. Don't worry so much." He finished the beer and wiped his mouth. "Let's go."

Having to borrow a bag for his wedding trip was a sore point with Ralph; he'd much rather have bought one of his own. There was a fine one displayed in the window of a luggage shop they passed every night on their way to the subway—a big, tawny Gladstone with a zippered compartment on the side, at thirty-nine, ninety-five—and Ralph had had his eye on it ever since Easter time. "Think I'll buy that," he'd told Eddie, in the same offhand way that a day or so before he had announced his engagement ("Think I'll marry the girl"). Eddie's response to both remarks had been the same: "Whaddya—crazy?" Both times Ralph had said, "Why not?" and in defense of the bag he had added, "Gonna get married, I'll *need* somethin' like that." From then on it was as if the bag, almost as much as Gracie herself, had become a symbol of the new and richer life he sought. But after the ring and the new clothes and all the other expenses, he'd found at last that he couldn't afford it; he had settled for the loan of Eddie's, which was similar but cheaper and worn, and without the zippered compartment.

Now as they passed the luggage shop he stopped, caught in the grip of a reckless idea. "Hey wait awhile, Eddie. Know what I think I'll do with that fifty-dollar bonus? I think I'll buy that bag right now." He felt breathless.

"Whaddya—crazy? Forty bucks for a bag you'll use maybe one time a year? Ya crazy, Ralph. C'mon."

"Ah—I dunno. Ya think so?"

"Listen, you better *keep* ya money, boy. You're gonna *need* it."

"Ah—yeah," Ralph said at last. "I guess ya right." And he fell in step with Eddie again, heading for the subway. This was the way things usually turned out in his life; he could never own a bag like that until he made a better salary, and he accepted it—just as he'd accepted without question, after the first thin sigh, the knowledge that he'd never possess his bride until after the wedding.

The subway swallowed them, rattled and banged them along in a rocking, mindless trance for half an hour, and disgorged them at last into the cool early evening of Queens.

Removing their coats and loosening their ties, they let the breeze dry their sweated shirts as they walked. "So, what's the deal?" Eddie asked. "What time we supposed to show up in this Pennsylvania burg tomorra?"

"Ah, suit yourself," Ralph said. "Any time in the evening's okay."

"So whadda we do then? What the hell can ya *do* in a hillbilly town like that, anyway?"

"Ah, I dunno," Ralph said defensively. "Sit around and talk, I guess; drink beer with Gracie's old man or somethin'; I dunno."

"Jesus," Eddie said. "Some weekend. Big, big deal."

Ralph stopped on the sidewalk, suddenly enraged, his damp coat wadded in his fist. "Look, you bastid. Nobody's gonna *make* ya come, ya know—you or Marty or George or any a the rest of 'em. Get that straight. You're not doin' *me* no favors, unnastand?"

"Whatsa matta?" Eddie inquired. "Whatsa matta? Can'tcha take a joke?"

"Joke," Ralph said. "You're fulla jokes." And plodding sullenly in Eddie's wake, he felt close to tears.

They turned off into the block where they both lived, a double row of neat, identical houses bordering the street where they'd fought and loafed and played stickball all their lives. Eddie pushed open the front door of his house and ushered Ralph into the vestibule, with its homely smell of cauliflower and overshoes. "G'wan in," he said, jerking a thumb at the closed living-room door, and he hung back to let Ralph go first.

Ralph opened the door and took three steps inside before it hit him like a sock on the jaw. The room, dead silent, was packed deep with grinning, red-faced men—Marty, George, the boys from the block, the boys from the office—everybody, all his friends, all on their feet and poised motionless in a solid mass. Skinny Maguire was crouched at the upright piano, his spread fingers high over the keys, and when he struck the first rollicking chords they all roared into song, beating time with their fists, their enormous grins distorting the words:

> *"Fa he's a jally guh fella*
> *Fa he's a jally guh fella*
> *Fa he's a jally guh fell-ah*
> *That nobody can deny!"*

Weakly Ralph retreated a step on the carpet and stood there wide-eyed, swallowing, holding his coat. *"That nobody can deny!"* they sang, *"That nobody can deny!"* And as they swung into the second chorus Eddie's father appeared through the dining-room curtains, bald and beaming, in full song, with a great glass pitcher of beer in either hand. At last Skinny hammered out the final line:

"That–no–bod–dee–can–dee–nye!"

And they all surged forward cheering, grabbing Ralph's hand, pounding his arms and his back while he stood trembling, his own voice lost under the noise. "Gee, fellas—thanks. I—don't know what to—thanks, fellas. . . ."

Then the crowd cleaved in half, and Eddie made his way slowly down the middle. His eyes gleamed in a smile of love, and from his bashful hand hung the suitcase—not his own, but a new one: the big, tawny Gladstone with the zippered compartment on the side.

"Speech!" they were yelling. *"Speech! Speech!"*

But Ralph couldn't speak and couldn't smile. He could hardly even see.

At ten o'clock Grace began walking around the apartment and biting her lip. What if he wasn't coming? But of course he was coming. She sat down again and carefully smoothed the billows of nylon around her thighs, forcing herself to be calm. The whole thing would be ruined if she was nervous.

The noise of the doorbell was like an electric shock. She was halfway to the door before she stopped, breathing hard, and composed herself again. Then she pressed the buzzer and opened the door a crack to watch for him on the stairs.

When she saw he was carrying a suitcase, and saw the pale seriousness of his face as he mounted the stairs, she thought at first that he knew; he had come prepared to lock the door and take her in his arms. "Hello, darling," she said softly, and opened the door wider.

"Hi, baby." He brushed past her and walked inside. "Guess I'm late, huh? You in bed?"

"No." She closed the door and leaned against it with both hands holding the doorknob at the small of her back, the way heroines close doors in the movies. "I was just—waiting for you."

He wasn't looking at her. He went to the sofa and sat down, holding the suitcase on his lap and running his fingers over its surface. "Gracie," he said, barely above a whisper. "Look at this."

She looked at it, and then into his tragic eyes.

"Remember," he said, "I told you about that bag I wanted to

buy? Forty dollars?" He stopped and looked around. "Hey, where's Martha? She in bed?"

"She's gone, darling," Grace said, moving slowly toward the sofa. "She's gone for the whole weekend." She sat down beside him, leaned close, and gave him Martha's special smile.

"Oh yeah?" he said. "Well anyway, listen. I said I was gonna borrow Eddie's bag instead, remember?"

"Yes."

"Well, so tonight at the White Rose I siz, 'C'mon, Eddie, let's go home pick up ya bag.' He siz, 'Ah, bag schmagg.' I siz, 'Whatsa matta?' but he don't say nothin', see? So we go home to his place and the living-room door's shut, see?"

She squirmed closer and put her head on his chest. Automatically he raised an arm and dropped it around her shoulders, still talking. "He siz, 'G'ahead, Ralph, open the door.' I siz, 'Whatsa deal?' He siz, 'Never mind, Ralph, open the door.' So I open the door, and oh Jesus." His fingers gripped her shoulder with such intensity that she looked up at him in alarm.

"They was all there, Gracie," he said. "All the fellas. Playin' the piana, singin', cheerin'—" His voice wavered and his eyelids fluttered shut, their lashes wet. "A big surprise party," he said, trying to smile. "Fa me. Can ya beat that, Gracie? And then—and then Eddie comes out and—Eddie comes out and hands me this. The very same bag I been lookin' at all this time. He bought it with his own money and he didn't say nothin', just to give me a surprise. 'Here, Ralph,' he siz. 'Just to let ya know you're the greatest guy in the world.'" His fingers tightened again, trembling. "I cried, Gracie," he whispered. "I couldn't help it. I don't think the fellas saw it or anything, but I was cryin'." He turned his face away and worked his lips in a tremendous effort to hold back the tears.

"Would you like a drink, darling?" she asked tenderly.

"Nah, that's all right, Gracie. I'm all right." Gently he set the suitcase on the carpet. "Only, gimme a cigarette, huh?"

She got one from the coffee table, put it in his lips and lit it. "Let me get you a drink," she said.

He frowned through the smoke. "Whaddya got, that sherry wine? Nah, I don't like that stuff. Anyway, I'm fulla beer." He leaned back and closed his eyes. "And then Eddie's mother feeds us this terrific meal," he went on, and his voice was almost normal now. "We had *steaks;* we had French-fried *potatas*"—his head rolled on the sofa-back with each item of the menu—"lettuce-and-tomato *salad, pickles, bread, butter*—everything. The works."

"Well," she said. "Wasn't that nice?"

"And afterwards we had ice cream and coffee," he said, "and all the beer we could drink. I mean, it was a real spread."

Grace ran her hands over her lap, partly to smooth the nylon and partly to dry the moisture on her palms. "Well, that certainly was nice of them," she said. They sat there silent for what seemed a long time.

"I can only stay a minute, Gracie," Ralph said at last. "I promised 'em I'd be back."

Her heart thumped under the nylon. "Ralph, do you—do you like this?"

"What, honey?"

"My negligee. You weren't supposed to see it until—after the wedding, but I thought I'd—"

"Nice," he said, feeling the flimsy material between thumb and index finger, like a merchant. "Very nice. Wudga pay fa this, honey?"

"Oh—I don't know. But do you like it?"

He kissed her and began, at last, to stroke her with his hands. "Nice," he kept saying. "Nice. Hey, I like this." His hand hesitated at the low neckline, slipped inside and held her breast.

"I do love you, Ralph," she whispered. "You know that, don't you?"

His fingers pinched her nipple, once, and slid quickly out again. The policy of restraint, the habit of months was too strong to break. "Sure," he said. "And I love you, baby. Now you be a good girl and get ya beauty sleep, and I'll see ya in the morning. Okay?"

"Oh, Ralph. Don't go. Stay."

"Ah, I promised the fellas, Gracie." He stood up and straightened his clothes. "They're waitin' fa me, out home."

She blazed to her feet, but the cry that was meant for a woman's appeal came out, through her tightening lips, as the whine of a wife: "Can't they wait?"

"Whaddya—*crazy?*" He backed away, eyes round with righteousness. She would *have* to understand. If this was the way she acted before the wedding, how the hell was it going to be afterwards? "Have a *heart,* willya? Keep the fellas waitin' *tonight?* After all they done fa *me?*"

After a second or two, during which her face became less pretty than he had ever seen it before, she was able to smile. "Of course not, darling. You're right."

He came forward again and gently brushed the tip of her chin with his fist, smiling, a husband reassured. " 'At's more like it," he said. "So I'll see ya, Penn Station, nine o'clock tomorra. Right, Gracie? Only, before I go—" he winked and slapped his belly. "I'm fulla beer. Mind if I use ya terlet?"

When he came out of the bathroom she was waiting to say goodnight, standing with her arms folded across her chest, as if for warmth. Lovingly he hefted the new suitcase and joined her at the door. "Okay, then, baby," he said, and kissed her. "Nine o'clock. Don't forget, now."

She smiled tiredly and opened the door for him. "Don't worry, Ralph," she said. "I'll be there."

— They don't have meeting ground.

— both of them will make the mistakes.

THE CONCEPTS
OF FICTION

6

UNITY

We learn an inestimable amount about how to write from our reading. By emulating models we can learn many devices for unifying our own material. But there remains much that we cannot learn from anyone else. And one overwhelming challenge haunts every honest writer every time he begins a new story. *How shall he conceive the unity of his work?*

This may seem like a minor or elusive problem. For the critic or the general reader it may be so. For the writer it may be elusive—maddeningly so—but it will not be minor. He knows that conceiving an overall unity is just about the same as determining for what ends he will use the fictional devices at his command. It is the *conception* that tells him what to include, what to leave out, where to start, and when to round out his conclusion. It must guide him in the selection and manipulation of all the elements of fiction from which he hopes to fashion a story.

If one were content merely to imitate a story already in print there would be no problem. But we want to—in the final analysis we *have* to—imitate life. And life, unhappily, provides far more examples of confusion and multiplicity than of unity.

Probably only birth and death represent any clear-cut terminals in actual life—and it is unthinkable that all stories should begin with a birth and end with a death. Furthermore, consistency in life is almost accidental. The thoughts and emotions of ten o'clock in the morning are almost certain to be followed by distractions at eleven. Insignificant distractions? Not at all. When we think about the matter honestly, we realize that no distraction is insignificant. In life everything is influenced by everything else. There are no neat, persistent patterns in the surface of life. If there were they would not stand still so we could copy them.

Life is a constant flux, and even one man's experience is full of chaotic diversions, inconclusive fadings away, and reappearances that seem more like new beginnings than ends.

In a lot of fiction, the conflicts of courtship end with a marriage. The courtship is given an appearance of unity by such a termination. The object that was sought consistently through courtship has been achieved. Why not end one's own story where many stories have ended?

Why not? Because the honestly troubled writer, fumbling for his own conception of a story that will imitate life, remembers that life didn't pause for the flicker of an eyelash when the bride said, "I do." Life stumbled and surged on, carrying away or rearranging all artificial boundaries. Before there is time to write of it, the marriage that seemed to mark the end of an epoch seems even more emphatically to mark the beginning of another—or to be merely another event in an endless sequence of events.

I am not trying to raise a philosophical quibble in emphasizing this discrepancy between unbounded life and the unity required in fiction. I am talking about something we are obliged to feel with a kind of desperation each time we begin to transpose experience into fiction.

The writer possesses, or is possessed by, deeply understood experience. He knows he has "something to say." He has some technical abilities to say it. But what—exactly what—is "it"? Ah, if life only presented itself to us in neatly measured chunks, each one wrapped and sealed so there would be no blending of one sort of experience with another. . . .

He is tempted to shout at all the mocking powers of the universe that you cannot imitate the formlessness of life by giving it any form at all.

Yet he knows he has to make certain tentative decisions about where to begin and end—from which side and level to cut into his material—if he is going to write at all. In one fashion or another he has to say, "Once upon a time. . . ." And this arbitrary declaration (which means "what I have to tell you began exactly *here*") must be followed by a statement of the situation prevailing when "*it all began.*" He has to begin to *impose* unity on raw material that has none.

It is in choosing how to impose unity that a writer declares or surrenders his independence. Here he chooses to follow a formula— which might have been very good for someone else's story—or invent a form that will be truly responsible to the still shapeless material that is his alone. The way in which he will impose unity on disorder determines whether or not his work will be really an imitation of life.

If he chooses independence (rather than formula) he still cannot begin his imposition of unifying devices nor his selection of material to imitate life as it appears to him when he contemplates it disinterestedly. He must start by imitating it as it appears when it is focused by emotion. So if he cares and cares deeply about his subject he has an initial advantage. Though life may appear an endless flux to the speculative mind, an emotional involvement makes it appear unified around (before and after) a momentary crisis.

The writer of an original story begins to shape his material by accepting an emotional commitment to it—very much as if he himself were the first character to appear in the story to be. This primary commitment is usually no more than scaffolding. It will be totally replaced by structural elements of the story itself before the story is done. But it offers an initial base for selecting one sort of character rather than another to play the principal role, for selecting one kind of conflict rather than another to demonstrate what truly was in issue, and for selecting a central action or plot to show what values triumphed and what ones lost as the conflict progressed.

Pure experience asks, What do I mean? The writer's first answer is, You mean what I *want* you to mean. So give me *this* character, *that* situation, and *those* possibilities of action to start with—no others, please—and I will show everyone what you meant to me.

This passionate wish to *make* experience yield a particular meaning is the heart of the creative act, the initial selection from which subsequent choices flow with an increasingly rational justification. The finishing touches on a story, the final impositions of unity, may be made as coldly, logically, conventionally as you wish. The first choices to cut into experience must be irrational and emotional—just exactly *as if* you were a character in your story, preferring one thing to another simply because you are yourself and want what you want out of a bewildering world.

This is the way the creative act of writing a story begins, but I have not meant to imply that one must complete a self-conscious and exhaustive examination of his soul before he begins each story. The primary choice of a way to segment experience is no doubt generally made by habit. It is one's second nature to admit some ready-made unities in experience and to accept them unquestioningly. One says automatically—if not quite correctly—"Oh, I know where the conflict began for the people I mean to write about. I'll start at that beginning." That's fine when it works. It's an example, perhaps, of the author unconsciously playing a character, exercising his prejudices to give a preliminary unity to his material.

And of course there are some subjects in which a natural unity is more readily apparent than in others. If your subject is to be the visit of a mysterious stranger, then what is more simple than to begin the story with his arrival and conclude it with his departure? The unity of many fine stories seems to have been given the author by those unifying labels we use in ordinary life: a visit, a love affair, a contest, a disaster, a journey, or a celebration.

Any writer with good common sense will respect these "given" unities when he can. I have not been probing the mysteries of how a writer begins to unify his work with the intent of recommending something fancy and profound instead of what is candid and easy.

Whenever there is an easy way to do something—and do it right—by all means prefer the easy way. Heaven knows, there are enough infinitely difficult things about writing so that one deserves any free throws he gets.

Bringing a story along the way from a first conception to completed form has often struck me as an ungainly progress. First the chosen material dictates. Among other things, it dictates certain unities which the writer is well-advised to accept.

Then comes the point at which the writer must dictate to his material.

The writer is pushed, then he pulls. The material regains its momentum. It pushes again. The writer pulls again. This makes for progress toward a good story—when the writer and the material move in the same direction. So it's up to the writer to keep his eyes open and his mind nimble when he takes his turn at supplying momentum, for the material is blind and incapable of making alternate choices. It is incapable of reinforcing unities when the inherent ones prove insufficient.

Plot, character, tone, and theme may all be adapted as the composition progresses, with the object of enhancing the unity of a story. A unified point of view, a unified set of symbols, and a disciplined consistency of language may be imposed by the author as it becomes increasingly clear to him what qualities must be stressed and which excluded from the subject that was in his first conception so indefinite in outline.

Plot unifies by disciplining the action. In forming a plot we ask not only what kinds of action might the characters have performed, but which of those actions would have direct bearing on the outcome of the story.

In "The Best of Everything," for example, the author might well have imagined a number of interesting episodes involving Grace and her roommate, Martha. Because of differences in temperament there is potential for significant conflict in almost every aspect of their lives together. Can't you imagine that Martha might have borrowed money from Grace, or have wanted Grace to stay away sometimes when she was entertaining boyfriends in their apartment? Yet, obeying the demands of the plot, Yates has wisely ruled out any such episodes, and we can see that they would be irrelevant.

Character unifies by requiring a concentration on the significance an act or condition has to a particular person at a particular time in his or her life. "Taking Care" begins with the statement that Jones has "been in love all his life"—yet the whole life of this aging man is far too broad a subject for a short story. Therefore, to show what his lifetime of humble devotion has amounted to the author concentrates on a period when Jones is threatened with the loss of his wife—for at this point of stress the qualities that have always been present in him are most sharply in view. The circumstances conceived by the author might be seen almost as a laboratory test designed to isolate and magnify characteristics that have often been harder to discern.

The tone of "Us He Devours" is achieved by a concentration of Miss Festner's inner life and is sustained by language indicative of her infatuation and alienation from the world of common social intercourse. Any matter-of-fact commentary on her habits, her work at the bank, or her small talk with associates would rupture the unity of the tale. Such things need not and should not be part of it.

The grotesque or absurd entanglements Murphy weaves for himself in "Murphy's Xmas" add up to a delicately qualified thematic statement about the nature of "death in life."

In the next chapters these unifying elements will be examined in more detail.

7

PLOT AS UNITY

Since each of us began to read fiction we have known what plot is. Alas, we seem to know it is different things.

Somehow among readers and critics—and among teachers of fiction writing, too—there have grown up "pro-plot" and "anti-plot" factions. The pro-plot people are bent on condemning fiction that, according to their measure, lacks plot. (It is distressing to find that by *plot* they often mean no more than a particular plot, often closely associated with a standard kind of subject. For instance, in a western story, unless the plot involves a conflict between a gunslinging stranger and a corrupt, wealthy landowner, there might appear to be no plot at all.)

The anti-plot people contend that plot is a mechanism that destroys the life in sound fictional material. They are right only in that this *sometimes* happens. Of course it need not. When plot is properly integrated with the overall unity, it can be first among those elements that give the illusion of life to fiction. For people are actors. Their nature is action.

And plot—plot is no more and no less than a causal sequence of action.

Note that it is not a mere sequence. We have no plot when we say, "Bertha tinted her hair red. That night she dined alone." We have a plot—or rather the small beginnings of one—when we say, "Being too timid to let her friends see that she had dyed her hair,

Bertha dined alone that night." The causal connection between dyeing the hair and dining alone is established in the second example as it is not in the first.

Yet we must note, and be very clear about it, that the causal connection between parts of the whole plot action is very often not stated explicitly. When we outline a plot in isolation from a story, the connections will probably be obvious. When we integrate a plot with other elements, the connections will often be shown indirectly, principally by the altering situation, intent, or emotion of the characters.

In a story like "Murphy's Xmas" the many excitements (and riddles) on the surface might distract us from the realization that it has a functioning plot. It will help to isolate and examine the plot if we make a distinction between what can be called the true chronology of events and the sequence in which these are presented by the finished fiction. That is, in the case of flashbacks or allusions to the past, consider these in proper calendar sequence when you're looking for the chain of causality that leads to the denouement. We must make a paraphrase, untangling that which is very properly woven into the fabric as we have it on the page.

Consider: The causal sequence in "Murphy's Xmas" begins with a long-drawn period of quarreling between husband and wife (merely alluded to in the text, not given in detail), during which Murphy established a relation with the younger woman, Annie.

Because Murphy and his wife had agreed to divorce, some of the guards they had raised against each other were lowered, *so* Murphy agreed to the intercourse which made her pregnant for the second time. This may seem like paradoxical motivation to innocent readers. But, however hard to accept, it is the motivation *given* for the act that leads to this complication of Murphy's passionate life.

Because Murphy is convinced that his wife has tricked him by getting pregnant again, their quarreling has a new dimension of bitterness on the trip home to Illinois. Murphy feels a special injustice in being separated from Annie and being forced to keep some semblance of appearances for the sake of the families they plan to visit.

Because this sense of injustice plays on his already exacerbated feelings, Murphy quarrels more violently with his father than he might have and is more than normally suspicious of Annie's fidelity to him. *So* these distresses drive him to the point where, once again, he has intercourse with his alienated wife. (Again this motivation may seem paradoxical. It is certainly irrational behavior—but let it be understood that it is one of the chief tasks of fiction to expose the unconscious will that makes the important determinations in life; that truly does overrule the best laid plans of mice and men.)

Finally, *because* Murphy has been driven to such fruitless attempts at consolation and been humiliated in his own eyes by his inability to direct his destiny rationally, we come to the important point of revelation, the "death in life" to which he is fated. Readers may wish to compare this thematic accomplishment of the plot with the statement at the end of James Joyce's story "Araby," in which the narrator realizes himself to be "driven and derided by vanity."

After we sense the natural "rounding out"—the unity—of some passage of causally related action, we see that its part in the general unity of the story comes from its relation to the needs, desires, and purposeful or capricious choices of characters. The original step in the action of a plot very frequently comes as the response of a character to the situation he must confront. The stimulus provoking the response is what we call motivation.

The significance and complexity of *motivation* may cover a vast range of intensity. If my leg itches, I am moved to scratch it. If Othello becomes suspicious of his wife, he is moved to resolve his suspicions and know the truth. But however important or unimportant the motive, we can hardly think of the action of a plot without acknowledging that it proceeds *through* the passionate decision of characters.

This is true whether the author chooses to use much space in examining the motives of his characters or leaves them to be inferred by the reader. We must never judge the profundity of fiction merely by the author's profundity in examining motives. Their best usage is in serving as the link between character and action. The question of how much motivation the author must supply seems to me best answered by the answer to another question: How much is needed to make the action proceed meaningfully out of the characters?

Criticism—and this means your judgment as you are writing a story as well as your estimate of someone else's work—must draw some fine measurements in determining sufficient motivation for a plot action. We know from personal experience that some things seem to "just happen." These include not only the things that happen to us, but those actions for which we must assume full responsibility before the law and before God. Not all of life, by any means, is shaped by those actions we undertake because we have a reason to. Yet, at the other extreme, the picture of an action that unrolls without being checked or furthered by the full choice of one or more characters seems altogether inhuman and therefore not the proper concern of fiction.

There are absolutely no prescriptions for the proper degree of motivation in any particular story. At the misty border where character melts into action and action stimulates changes in character, the author has a particular responsibility for declaring his own view of life. In Thomas Hardy's novels, motives do not count for much against the sweep of an impersonal fate that drives his characters against their will. (In *Jude the Obscure* the chief character quotes Aeschylus: "Things are as they are and will proceed to their destined end." What people may wish or attempt will have little consequence, Hardy seems to say in most of his novels.)

I am afraid it is not so easy to find, in the literature of this century, examples of the opposite extreme. The effectiveness of the personal will is not a theme to which most contemporary writers incline. But it is possible to find, in the novels of Jane Austen, Dickens, or George Eliot, a considerably closer tie between personal motive and the consequence of action.

Often plots are praised for their "inevitability." This means the reader is convinced that if event *A* took place it is nearly unthinkable that it should not have been followed by *B*. Once *B* has happened, then *C* must follow. Now of course any writer is in a position to be skeptical of the inevitability of any plot. He knows that after he has written *A* into his story, he could follow it with *E* or *J*—with *K* or *X*. At a certain point of composition when his materials were still fluid in his mind, the arrangement of events could be determined by pure whim.

Yes—at a certain point. The same is true of love. "Love has no conscience," says one of Shakespeare's sonnets. It may, as well as not, begin with a whimsical choice. "But who does not know that conscience comes from love?" The reasons for a whimsical choice in love or in forming a fictional plot begin to develop *after* a choice is made. And you will find that they assert themselves with ever more rigor as the various elements begin to fall into place.

All the elements in a story must be, as it were, "consulted" before the writer dares make certain decisions required to give the finished shape to his plot. He makes some initial declarations, arising from his conception. He writes down that his characters have done something. But then he pauses to consider who these characters are and what they might *want* to do next.

Yet, in urging pauses for consultation, I don't mean that characters can be allowed to dictate their own fates. There are writers who say, "I begin by creating characters. When they come to life, they write the story for me." I doubt if this is ever quite the whole truth. If it were, such a method could probably not result in a unified piece of fiction.

Characters make their own demands. So do other elements. But against all these pressures (never ignoring them) the mind of the author goes on urging the demands for continuity and unity of the plot. One requirement is pitted against another, and the story grows the way a vase rises on a potter's wheel, with one hand inside and one outside, both helping to determine the form.

It is not the pressure for a plot, but that pressure plus whatever in the material resists it with its own demands that results in the best plots.

When a writer's intuition tells him that what *is* happening to himself as he imaginatively shares the peril of his characters *would* be the next thing to befall them, he is in a position to reveal the deepest truth he knows by shaping the plot according to this intuition.

8

CHARACTER

In real life, character is revealed to us; in fiction, character is created. *There* is the difference between experience and artifice.

One begins by drawing from life. The writer knows or has known some actual person whose qualities suit the role left open for someone in his general concept of a story.

We know that a great number of the best fictional characters have been drawn from life. Biographers delight in telling us which members of the family, which friends, and which enemies served as models for great authors. In *Anna Karenina* Kitty is drawn from Tolstoy's wife. Emily Bronte drew her brother Branwell in creating the character of Heathcliff in *Wuthering Heights*. Surely Flaubert used his mistress Louise Colet as a model for the portrait called Madame Bovary. In the gallery of autobiographical characters, Levin is Tolstoy's self-portrait. Stephen Dedalus is Joyce's.

All this is true, as far as it goes—and it doesn't go far enough to satisfy the writer confronted with the problem of how to get Uncle Harry—or himself—onto the white sheets of paper lying beside his typewriter. You can't just press the old boy onto the paper, like a rose pressed between the pages of a book. And a typewriter isn't a camera. You can't get a portrait just by pressing one of the little nickeled levers

We've got to ask what it means when we use the figurative expression "drawing from life." It means first of all observing a person, noting his history and his appearance, his bank roll and his mustache. It means achieving, to the extent we can, some sense of identification with that person so we know, intuitively, what it means to him when he says "I." Though scholarship has determined who is the principal model Flaubert used in writing of the adulterous wife of a country doctor, we would know much too little about the process of creation if we could not grasp what Flaubert meant by saying, *"Madame Bovary, c'est moi."* ("I am Madame Bovary.") He meant that he had passed from observation of externals to a personal, intuitive knowledge of "I" as a desperate woman.

After observation and (when possible) a kind of identification, one still has to do more than feed the results of experience into a story like sand fed into a bag. We must not suppose that Louise Colet was the only model for Emma Bovary. Several other women contributed, including the unfortunate wife of a country doctor who had been, in reality, a student of Flaubert's father. From one woman the author drew mouth, eyes, insecurity, and the tendency to daydream, we suppose. From another he got those memorable fingernails and an unruly temper. From still another came the body and the outrageously trusting naiveté.

A fictional character—and particularly one who occupies a central position in a sizable work—is a composite, then, like so many of the other elements in fiction.

What determines which are suitable among all the characteristics available to a writer with a good memory and several models for a single character? Well, the plot, for one thing, gives some useful indications of what is required in a particular role and what is inappropriate. That is, if the plot requires a woman to cuckold her husband with a vain ladies' man, it must be obvious that the woman can't be given characteristics of tranquillity, obedience, or good sense. She has to emerge as the composite of those characteristics that would make such an action seem probable, and only those.

It is not necessary to think of plot as a dictatorial preconception imposed by the author to see that it always acts as a shaping and selecting influence in the development of characters. In some stories it is evident that characters have been mutilated to fit plot requirements. Obviously this is bad art. But even when it takes form at the same pace as the characters grow, plot restrains, limits, and gives definition to those characters.

The qualities of a character are also selected and shaded by the rest of the cast. The adulterous wife must be made to fit with the particular husband assigned her by the story, and with the particular seducer. In developing the whole cast of characters for his story, the author is a bit like a hostess planning a party, inviting guests who complement each other. The author has, though, the privilege and obligation of literally shaping the people he wants— not merely exercising a hostess's tact and judgment.

But, given an original conception of character and certain limiting requirements within the structure of the story, still more is required to make the artifice of fiction *seem* a true reflection of life. There ought to be in a story some quality of decision that will give the illusion that the characters are acting on their own volition. In "The Lady with the Pet Dog" Gurov is "already" bored with Anna after their first adultery. Yet the very naiveté and remorse that seem so boring in the woman are the qualities that will presently make him fall in love with her "really, truly—for the first time in his life." It amuses him that she considers him, at first, to be "kind, exceptional, high-minded" when he has treated her with the "coarse arrogance of a happy male . . . twice her age." Yet he will seek his own humility in an attempt to become what she erroneously thought him to be.

We can explain these expressive, ironic turns in the story by saying that the author's observation of life had shown him similar ironies. And we know that Chekhov "made things turn out" as he did to express the discrepancy between a man's superficial intentions and his underlying will. There is, beyond doubt, the imposition of a preconceived design on the material of this story. And yet it conveys to us the illusion of life because we feel that in the course of writing it Chekhov underwent the change of emotions that he attributes to Gurov—that the nice, bearded, passionate author at his desk must have said, "But after all *I* love Anna for the very qualities that amused me in the beginning."

One senses that almost magical (and yet common) submersion of the author's identity in the identity of his chief character. Logic and intellect and practice as a writer are all superseded while the author believes, "*I am Gurov.* What I have been doing in permitting him the action that has taken place thus far in my story is permitting myself that action. Next *I* will do this. . . .*"*

Of course no author ever completely gives up his own identity in the creative process. Chekhov knows he is Chekhov even when he chooses as Gurov. And when he has finished playing Gurov's role, he will look back over his work with the cold eye of the craftsman—striking out one passage and adding a calculated effect to polish his story. But unless he has known the moment of identification, when author and character are one, his labors of revision will be partly wasted.

It is probably these moments of identification that weld character and plot together in a perfect fusion, even if each has come from a separate process of thought, even if the plot was loosely determined a week before the character was settled on. Without such fusions, fiction is something less than art.

So, wouldn't it be wonderful if identification of author and character guaranteed perfect fiction? But it might mean only that the writer had perfected a way of daydreaming on paper. When the author is Chekhov—a conscious master of his craft who knows very well how to mesh the elements of his story before he yields conscious control—great fiction results. In the case of a writer who has not yet learned how to mingle character and action in a design of language, identification is often no better than self-indulgence.

Let's go back from the pinnacle of the art to some fundamentals. It is fundamental for the writer to remember that:

1. A character in a story is an artificial construction.
2. A character is composed by certain combinations of the basic elements of fiction—language, descriptions, actions, dialogue, and interaction with scene and other characters.
3. A fictional character is not alive in the same sense a human being is, but in a parallel sense. The character "lives" in the environment that the author builds for him, not in the limitless world of actuality.

Let's illustrate these points by reference to the stories included in this book.

Consider the weirdly stylized character of Miss Festner in "Us He Devours"—the spinster with "hard breasts" and "quick money-counting fingers." Accepting such details as being in accord with reality as he has experienced it, the reader still does not really ask, "*Was* there such a woman somewhere on this earth, once upon a time?" He believes that there *is* such a person because the author has temporarily forced him to accept the artificial world of the story as the only reality that concerns him.

Murphy's dumb, delicious Annie ("Murphy's Xmas") is not a real girl. We will never see her. We will only see words on a printed page. But we will remember her *as if* we had seen her because Mr. Costello built up an artificial association of girl with *shy skeleton, her thighs so cool, the pearl flick of her tongue,* and the way her fingers *make star-shaped wrinkles in the sheets* when a man presses her down onto a bed.

These words call to my mind images as moving as anything in my personal memory—but I know that if Costello had been making lilies out of crepe paper, wire, and wax he would not be producing objects more artificial than his story.

I stress the artificiality of fiction and the comparison with the flower maker because it is important to remember that writing fiction *ends* in a construction resembling nature, just as flower-making does. No one praises badly made artificial flowers just because their maker understood the horticulture of real plants. Similarly, a story cannot be praised merely because the author *started* from sound observation of human character.

Observation of character is structured into fiction by various kinds of description. In first person narration the narrator often defines himself and his motives. "I loved her ignorantly, impurely, and intermittently, sometimes unfurling toward her passions that . . . were, no doubt, more appropriate when directed toward building model airplanes . . . etc." ("In the Central Blue"). Such characterizations depend for their credibility on the general credibility of the narrator, and it is a nice trick to shape him so the reader may be aware of his biases.

Jones the preacher is "like an animal in a traveling show who, through some aberration, wears a vital organ outside the skin. . . ." His daughter's fingernails "were crudely bitten, some bleeding below the quick. She was tough and remote, wanting only to go on a trip for which she had a ticket." His wife is "no longer a woman, the woman whom he loves, but a situation." And his granddaughter's eyes "are a foal's eyes, navy-blue. She has grown in a few weeks to expect everything from Jones." ("Taking Care"). These descriptions, of course, do not tell us all we know about Jones and his dependents. But they supplement and heighten what we learn of them by taking in the situation and relationships of the story.

" 'Isn't he funny?' " Grace's roommate says of her fiancé. " 'He says "terlet." I didn't know people really said "terlet." ' " ("The Best of Everything"). This scant and offhand description of Ralph by a girl who has had little chance to observe him may, indeed, do little by itself to characterize the husband-to-be for us. But, as it is structured into the story, it prepares us for the monstrous shock of revelation at the end. Then Ralph, in the full flowering of his callousness, will ask his bride, " 'Mind if I use ya terlet?' "—and the shocked reader will see that this man regards his woman as no more than a vessel into which he can relieve himself. Then, I suppose, we are in a position to grasp and evaluate his character.

An author's knowledge of his character is built into the story by the actions he is called on to perform, whether these actions contribute directly to the plot or not. When Murphy bashes his fist against one solid surface after another, we get a measure of his inner fury and inability to find an appropriate target for it. The plot action—Murphy's self-destructive returns to the embrace of his wife—reveals his character even more forcefully.

When the boy on the way home from the movie ("In the Central Blue") tries to neck the girl his treacherous friend is necking, some sort of post-pubescent frenzy is revealed in its full enormity. The afterthoughts on this episode supplied by the adult narrator are intended to emphasize rather than minimize the absurdity involved.

Gurov's trip to Anna's home town ("The Lady with the Pet Dog") establishes the irrationality underlying his agile intelligence and prefigures the victory of love over the sterile self-image he has trusted so long. The trip is essential to the advancement of the plot—but we know the plot could have been forced to the same conclusion by the use of some other episode. Of course the other possible plot linkages would have done less to round out an image of a particular sort of man discovering his fate than the one the author chose.

Dialogue has always seemed to me one of the indispensable devices for shading and particularizing a character. In real life we like to see a person's face and hear his actual voice before we judge what he is up to. Fictional dialogue can be made to render very sensitively the mental and emotional ingredients in characters whose general outlines have already been accounted for. Although the dialogue in "Murphy's Xmas" is not conventionally punctuated, the following passage will serve to illustrate its fundamental fidelity to the characters involved.

The shattered family is driving home from the holiday visit when the young son points a toy pistol at his father's head and asks:

Why don't you come back Daddy?

Before he can think or excuse himself, Murphy says, *Because.*

Because why?

Because Mommy and I fight.

You're not fighting now.

In tears and on her knees, Murphy's wife lunges into the back seat and disarms her son. But he begins to cry and find his ultimatum: Daddy

I'm too shy to have a new daddy. I want you to be my daddy, and if you won't come back and be my daddy

I'm going to kill you.

Here the degree of pain felt by each of the three members of the family is measured out, along with the degree of restraint and responsibility the two adults can call up to master it and preserve a semblance of rational behavior against the uninhibited threat from the child.

Almost every story contains a number of characters. Some of them are little more than names. Others have things to say, bits of action to perform. Some—frequently one or two in each story—are the excuse for the story's existence. We see events through their eyes, or see them as if we were riding on their shoulders. What they do, see, and feel is the meaning of the story.

To accept the illusion of the story, the reader needs to know these central characters pretty well. Insofar as the design of the story permits, they should be made into "round" characters. That is, we need to show not merely their primary passions and motivations, but some of the hesitations and equivocations that are not altogether lined up with their principal drives. This character wants to make a fortune. Good. That's his main drive. But he won't cut throats to do it. That complicates things. He is relentless in his ambition. But susceptible to the diversions of love. That too complicates things—and is, very briefly, what is meant by showing a character in the round.

Rounding a character obviously makes him more lifelike, therefore more interesting. So it would seem at first thought that the thing to do is round out and complicate every character in a story. To the extent that this is done, the story would be improved, wouldn't it?

No. It would spoil the design of the story, destroy the overall unity. Round characters are part of the design of a good story, but so are flat ones, characters in whom there is no complexity.

In "The Best of Everything" it adds to the story that Gracie is dubious of the marriage *and* determined to go through with it. That Ralph is sexually attracted to her *and* unable to recognize her invitation. Without such degrees of roundness the story would mean little. At the same time, to keep proportion, to allow Gracie and Ralph their place in the center of the scene, it is necessary that Mr. Atwood be left flat as a stereotype and that Eddie should appear as the single-minded oaf, without the depth or variety within his character that such a person might have in real life.

Obviously the problem of flat and round characters is different in novels than it is in short stories. The novel simply offers more space for the author to show the variety within his characters and, if he wants to, to develop more of them in the round than he could in a short story. But basically the principle is the same. Flat characters are required as foils for the ones more fully rounded.

Needless to say, flat characters should not be dull characters. In "The Lady with the Pet Dog" Gurov's wife is a stereotype of the Russian intellectual female of her day. Anna's husband is a "flunkey." The two of them hardly appear on the scene of the story. Yet they are rendered with such sharp observation that they are a significant part of the whole unity. They are exactly what they have to be to help us see Anna and Gurov and their motives for adultery.

Sometimes it seems that the minor, flat characters in short stories amount to no more than a single epithet—"the fat man," or "Mr. Beaver, the timid boarder," or "Helen—the watchful eye." Seeing that they are only puppets made of a few words—and that still they may give a sense of lifelikeness within the whole unity of the story—the writer is reminded of the most important fact about his craft.

All fictional characters are made up of words. Observation begins the process. Identification—acting out the part—carries it along. But finally it is choice of language, the artifice of design and relationship to other fictional elements, that makes the character live for the reader.

9

TONE

We know from ordinary conversational experience that the same episode, involving the same people, may be told in different ways, each of them producing a different effect on the hearer. The tone of the speaker's voice may be sarcastic or sympathetic, awed or contemptuous.

The use of tone in conversation is analagous to, but not entirely the same as, its use in creating fiction. The use of lighting effects in the theater is also analogous to the manipulation of fictional tone. The background music in movies is a similar device from another art. We know how emotional receptivity can be heightened by such music. The Indians are about to appear over the edge of the butte. Tense, rapid, loud, brassy music rouses all our memories of danger, fear of the unknown. The Indians charge down the slope clothed and armed with all the terrible weaponry that the audience can imagine for them.

Fiction lacks the powerful mechanical supplements of tone that the movies and the stage can draw on to set the imagination of the audience at work to help communicate the story. But fiction has the quiet, inexhaustible resources of language itself. Whatever the shape of plot or characters, an author has the duty as well as the opportunity of choosing language which will condition the reader's receptivity to them.

It seems useful to distinguish a number of ways in which language may be used to produce tonal effects.

First it produces them by an appeal to sentiments. Certain words will generally evoke sympathy for any object to which they are applied. Other words or combinations of words will evoke suspicion, distaste, or dismay. Obviously, when Ralph is called a worm—"a white worm" ("The Best of Everything"), or Anna's husband is called a "flunkey" ("The Lady with the Pet Dog"), the author expects the reader to respond with antipathy for these men. (Single labels like this are not, of course, final judgments on any fictional character. In fact, one of the tricks available to a writer is to rouse a preliminary antipathy for a character and then win the reader over to approval. Such play with the reader's responses is what I mean by *theatrical* maneuvering.)

The significance of labeling Ralph's friends as "the fellas" is not quite so obviously a cue for the reader to pass judgment. To call a group of friends "the fellas" is ordinarily innocuous enough. But in the context of the story (and the effect of words always depends on their fictional context) the innocuous sentimentality shows up as evidence of sexual and intellectual immaturity with sheer cruelty as its consequence. In using the cliché term "the fellas" the author has added a tonal effect to complement the meaning of the action.

Tonal effects in "Us He Devours" are absolutely essential to the complex ironies involved. Because we live in a secular age, the author had to be very careful to dissociate himself from any flat statement or implication that the Great God Pan exists—except in the frustrated yearnings of old ladies wasted by the routine of their jobs. And yet the possibility must be left open that just such unlikely persons may be the mystic seers who perceive realities to which the rest of us are blind. A most difficult balance had to be struck—so the reader will have the choice of interpreting the tone as mock heroic *or* solemnly ecstatic.

The following passage may illustrate the writer's cunning in seizing on the fringe of our superstitions and exploiting them by a type of hyperbole.

She heard once more the cry of the loon: near, then far away. She heard something hoarse, and very close in the ring of the briers. Held fast in the bondage of her desire, she lay with eyes closed in the moonlight, and still nothing came to her.

Over, she thought. Oh, over and gone and never again to return to me. . . . Then, like a reprieve the coarse odor came to her. The lust of its eye rustled the briers. . . .

In a frenzy she opened her gifts.

Against rocks she broke the expensive, sullen perfumes. Each vial shattered and split and this enticement by odor overwhelmed even the trunks of the black trees.

Oh, come to me?

Hyperbole is exaggeration. And if we pause to think rationally about the passage above, we will of course conclude that it is not literally true that when the perfume is spilled out "this enticement by odor overwhelmed even the trunks of the black trees." Common sense balks.

But under the spell of the heightened language, common sense has been superseded. The exaggeration seems more true than a flat statement—"Miss Festner's sensory perceptions were disordered"—would be. For Mr. Hall's language means that in the disorder of her sensory perceptions a vision of the world hidden to sense has become accessible to the ecstatic woman.

Exaggeration of the kind just pointed out is one of the perils—but also one of the richest potentialities—of the language we lump under the general heading of rhetoric. Rhetoric is "high-flown" language. It contains emotional overtones and suggestions not necessarily present in the objects or events it refers to. It "says more" than is required to convey the sensuous appearance of objective acts or things. The danger in its usage is that it may say so much that is superfluous to communication that the reader will take it for mere wind, mere indulgence of a large, sloppy vocabulary.

The opposite of rhetoric—but just as much a distortion of common-sense reporting—is understatement. As the term implies, it means the author has chosen a language so sparse, clipped, and uninflected that the reader is almost obliged to say of the events and characters described, "By gad, there must be more to this situation than meets the eye." And his imagination is provoked into supplying interpretations that the author's language steadfastly refuses.

The stylist who employs understatement works like a boxer who feints in order to draw a punch from his opponent. Then, if he is a real stylist, like Hemingway, after he has provoked the reader into action, he counterpunches. Just as much as the rhetorical writer, the understater means to control the imagination of his reader. Both are using tonal, theatrical effects.

Somewhere in the middle, between rhetoric and understatement, there is the undistorted style, the realm of language that neither exaggerates nor minimizes the values of the events that fiction presents.

Ah, you will say at last, the undistorted style must be the proper style for fiction.

But is it?

Not necessarily at all. The preeminent writers of American fiction in the first half of this century have been Hemingway and Faulkner. Faulkner's style is clearly a rhetorical one. Hemingway stands almost as the inventor of understatement. There has been much fine fiction in the "middle style," but nothing to quite compare with the work of these two.

It would be a sad day for fiction if the undistorted, "middle" style should lose its popularity. We would then not have enough fine stories like "The Best of Everything" or Chekhov's magnificent study of adultery. The principle, "the word should be the cousin to the deed"—which means calling a spade a spade, and neither "an implement of cultivation" (rhetoric) or a "thing" (understatement) —is the safest principle for fiction. Stylists who shun both rhetorical heightening and understatement seem to serve the principle most faithfully.

But they pay a price for their lukewarmness. They do without many—not all—of the tonal effects that are the subject of this chapter.

Of course rhetoric, middle style, and understatement can all serve the purposes of fiction. All can be abused.

When rhetoric is abused, the result is what we call "purple" or "false poetic" language—merely colorful language that hides the subject instead of revealing it by significant theatrical lighting.

A sense of propriety, a sense of tact must be developed to curb the abuses of one sort or another of theatrical, tonal exaggerations of language. To a large extent this tact will grow, at its own sweet pace, as you get more experience in reading. Caution might well be the watchword until tact has matured. To be on the safe side, the beginning writer probably ought to incline toward a middle style—choosing the language suggested by observation of his subject, and the language required to communicate the real substance of characters and their acts.

An author may make adaptations of plot solely to modulate tone. The shaping of a single character or the selection of a cast of characters may have an important effect on tone. The novels of Thomas Hardy (*Jude the Obscure, The Mayor of Casterbridge*) make good illustrations of both these propositions. The unmistakable note of grief—the lamentation of a helpless, compassionate observer of the human scene—that makes the novels so memorable would be weaker if the author had not forced into the plot some improbable excesses of disaster to heighten the reader's emotional response. We know the author is exaggerating when he forces *all* those disasters on Jude and Sue. But we catch the tone of compassion exactly because we note the exaggeration. As for the use of character to achieve the tone the author wants, note that the presence of good-humored, stalwart minor characters is a favorite Hardy device for modulating the grimness smothering the lives of his main characters.

Think how the tone (not to mention other elements) of Shakespeare's *Othello* would be altered if he had cast some of his other characters in the situation of that play. If Portia instead of Desdemona had married Othello. . . . Well, of course she might have argued him out of killing her for supposed adultery, but if she hadn't—if Othello had again been so maddened by Iago's lies that he must kill—the tone of the whole play would be different. It is precisely Desdemona's sweet submissiveness set in a contrast of opposition to Othello's rage of love that leaves a special tone ringing in our minds when we forget some of the actions of the plot.

10

THEME

Theme is the meaning of a story.

It is not the "moral." It is not the revelation made by the final action. It is not to be confused with subject matter.

It is what the author has to say about his subject matter. It is expressed by all the material and the formal devices incorporated into the story—that add up to the overall unity—but it is not exactly the same as this unity. It is related to the unity of a story as light is related to a light bulb. That is, theme *comes from* the unity of a story as light comes from a carefully made mechanical implement.

We would need to know little more than this about theme if we were reading for pleasure or reading as critics. (Though experience and attention would be required in order to grasp the theme of a well-done contemporary story.)

Since we are reading as writers, we want to understand as much as we can of how the pursuit of meaning—of theme—enters into the process of composition. What is its part in the imaginative effort that begins when an author chooses a subject?

In all probability, a vague, powerful glimpse of the meaning inherent in a subject was what led to the choice of that subject in the first place. (In Chapter 2 we began to examine the act of writing by comments on the choice of subject matter. Now we have spiraled back to considering what may precede that choice. Do you feel that we are progressing backward? Good. A writer's progress must be backward—toward the sources of his knowledge and imagination—as well as forward to a disciplined control of his craft.)

Purely for the sake of illustrating how theme may be both the beginning and end of the storytelling process, let me conjecture how "Us He Devours" *might have been* conceived—how its theme might first have risen in the author's mind. (Imagining the processes of another writer's imagination is a useful stretching exercise for our own.)

Mr. Hall is—let us suppose—turning the pages of a newspaper while he finishes his third cup of morning coffee. He pauses to chuckle over a story of how an old lady who appears to have led a flawless life is at last apprehended for long-term, systematic embezzlement from the bank where she works.

Why on earth—he asks himself in idle amusement—*why on earth* would such a person *need* to embezzle? Why, why why?

He does not set about to find a rational answer to this question. He has no practical responsibilities that require a rational explanation. His responsibilities, as a writer, are of a different sort—to entertain that residue of wonder and uncertainty that would remain in any case after the authorities had settled the matter to their satisfaction and explained it according to their routine requirements.

So—idly as it would appear to some—he lets the riddle of motivation soften, melt, dissolve among the riddles that are always there when we seek to know truly the roots of our own desires.

What anxieties or uncanny hopes are disguised beneath the rationalizations for our ordinary employment or our rebellions against its rules? What is the disguised object of all desire? Is all desire sexual at root? Religious? An amalgam of the two?

Now drifting far from the newspaper item that first sparked his curiosity, Mr. Hall may well turn over ultimate psychological and metaphysical stones. He may (for he is a man of letters, critic and poet as well as a fiction writer) ponder again a passage from Wallace Stevens' famous poem "Sunday Morning":

> *What is divinity if it can come*
> *Only in silent shadows and in dreams?*

Isn't the end of mortal longing a wish to behold the divinity with our trustable mortal senses? Isn't it, though, uncanny to suppose that a quiet, old lady bank teller might have looted her bank as a means of paying tribute to a god unknown to her community? Uncanny indeed—and there's the fun of it, the temptation to make a story that is unbelievable and yet, somehow, safe from disproof— the sort of story that our dreams tell us, coloring our minds with strange dyes even when we are not sure what to make of what they have said.

Somewhere among these cloudy, nebulous speculations, Mr. Hall may have decided . . . "she took the money for the sake of a goat"—a goat, as we know, being metaphorically associated with lust, witches' revels, Satan, and Pan. Myth, folklore, and dream validate the choice of an invisible goat as one of the characters in the story he is preparing to compose. The author knows as well as we that the goat figure is only acceptable in his metaphorical existence, and so he will prepare to project him only through the medium of Miss Festner's supercharged emotions. But, at any rate, once he has decided on the goat, he has fixed on the subject of his story.

It will be Miss Festner's last desperate gamble to make physical contact with that which has only manifested itself to her previously by signs and intimations. In the story will be Miss Festner's fervid dash into the darkened countryside, where she will try to lure the goat by spreading out her tributes to him and, finally, by disguising herself in the tempting pelt of a beast, "lowing" to the recalcitrant lord of her desires. It is quite possible that Mr. Hall thought of the myth of Queen Pasiphae and the White Bull from the Sea in formulating this episode. Part of his subject is also the ultimate reckless theft of cash from the bank, "in case it was money that was wanted, after all."

In the previous chapter I discussed the ways in which the use of language controlled the tone in bringing out the potentials of the subject matter. Here in another passage, let's consider how some words have been chosen to highlight subtly the religious aspect of Miss Festner's obsession, the imperatives that go beyond mere hunger for sensuous comfort or gratification. Ponder carefully the italicized items.

> She felt more deserted, and more forlorn, than ever before. Yet she was not and never could be *sinfully* passive, for urgency even in her waking hours grew like a fuse somewhere inside her. She recognized, she even welcomed, the desperation that came galloping into her. She knew she *must go out, must seek, must search once more.*

Now it must be plain that this language cannot have been fully formed in the author's mind at the moment he had his first intimation of what the story could mean. Of course the whole process of writing—formation of plot, characters, language, and all—is required to mature or ripen a theme. Nevertheless, the thematic intent must be present, in however unripened a form, to guide the mind of the writer through every stage of composition.

It is perhaps the most fundamental of the principles of selection indicating which one of the several choices an author must make from the possibilities open to him.

It has been persuasively argued that the theme of a story cannot ever be satisfactorily abstracted from the story itself. It is, I believe, always coarsened and flawed when it is abstracted. Properly speaking, the theme is what is left, like a resonance, in the reader's mind after he has recovered from the emotions and sympathies he felt while reading and even after he has forgotten the shape of the plot and the illusion of life contributed by the characters.

Nevertheless, purely for purposes of analysis—to pry open the imaginative structure of the stories so we can peer inside—I'll risk tentative statements of theme for each of the other stories in this book.

In the Central Blue says: The libidinous confusions of an adolescent boy teach him the painful cost of renouncing confusion. To "think straight" always requires some amputation of desire.

Taking Care says: Charity will see you through even when faith and hope are doused. (It's a marvel to me that this superficially "tough" story should disclose so traditional a Christian message after all.)

The Lady with the Pet Dog says: A man can stumble into the humility of love through the arrogance of lust. (Is there a similar theme in other stories or novels you have read recently? Can you write a story on a similar theme? Please don't make the error of writing anything merely to *illustrate* a theme, however wise or important that theme may sound to you. But if a theme from something you have read strikes a responsive spark in your imagination, tend the spark and see if it will light up into a story from your own experience.)

Murphy's Xmas says: Life is not so easily distinguished from death as we might like to believe.

The Best of Everything says: Marriage can be a doom as savage as a blood sacrifice in spite of the sentimentalities that accompany it. (Doesn't the relentless movement of the story toward the final disappointment suggest the passage of a condemned woman on her way to the place of punishment?)

It is possible, I suppose, to write a story without a theme, though I have suggested that stories often begin to shape in the writer's mind when the theme flickers into his consciousness. It is not only possible, but common, that the theme of a story may be shallow or commonplace. It is a good idea to review your own work a few days after it appears finished—after you've given your mind time to cool—and ask, "Does it mean anything?" Do you still find in it, approaching as a reader, that insistent spark of meaning from which the story sprang? Does the material really mean what it seemed to mean while you were in the heat of writing? It is by no means unusual for a writer to miss the potential significance of his work while he is busy putting it together. Part of the process of revision consists in probing for that significance by reading and considering one's second thoughts. The next step is to add whatever is required—another character, a more exactly chosen phrase, another step in the plot development, or a bit of narrative preparation—to heighten that significance.

A writer hopes to be neither obscure nor tactlessly insistent on a point that will seem mundane to his readers. I suppose that between these extremes it is better to be tactless than obscure, but both are faults that can be refined away by experience as writer and as critical reader of your own work. Maintain the habit of comparing your work with accomplished professional work—with the stories in this book, for example. Don't be too savage with yourself in making comparisons, and don't let your work off too easily. And realize that in this matter of theme—the ultimate statement of your story—perhaps nothing but a sensitive comparison will tell you how far you have succeeded.